The Journal of Andrew Fuller Studies

Published in the United States of America by
by The Andrew Fuller Center for Baptist Studies
The Southern Baptist Theological Seminary
2825 Lexington Road
Louisville, Kentucky 40280

© The Andrew Fuller Center for Baptist Studies 2021

All rights reserved. No part of this publication may be reproduced, stored in a retrieval system, or transmitted, in any form or by any means, without the prior permission in writing of The Andrew Fuller Center for Baptist Studies, or as expressly permitted by law, by license, or under terms agreed with the appropriate reproduction rights organization.

ISBN 978-1-77484-041-2

Printed by H&E Publishing, Peterborough, Ontario, Canada

The Journal of Andrew Fuller Studies

The *Journal of Andrew Fuller Studies* is an open access, double-blind peer-reviewed, scholarly journal published online biannually in February and September by the Andrew Fuller Center for Baptist Studies (under the auspices of The Southern Baptist Theological Seminary). The publication language of the journal is English. Articles that deal with the life, ministry, and thought of the Baptist pastor-theologian Andrew Fuller are very welcome, as well as essays on his friends, his Particular Baptist community in the long eighteenth century (1680s–1830s), and the global impact of his thought, known as "Fullerism."

Articles and book reviews are to follow generally the style of Kate L. Turabian, *A Manual for Writers of Research Papers, Theses, and Dissertations*, 9th ed. (Chicago: University of Chicago Press, 2018). They may be submitted in British, American, Australian, New Zealand, or Canadian English. Articles should be between 5,000 and 8,000 words, excluding footnotes. Articles are to be sent to the Editor and book reviews to the Book Review Editors.

Editor: Michael A G Haykin, FRHistS
Chair & Professor of Church History
& Director, The Andrew Fuller Center for Baptist Studies
The Southern Baptist Theological Seminary, Louisville, Kentucky
mhaykin@sbts.edu

Associate editors: Baiyu Andrew Song, PhD cand.
The Southern Baptist Theological Seminary
Louisville, Kentucky
& Part-time lecturer, Redeemer University, Ancaster, Ontario
bsong677@students.sbts.edu

Design editor: Dustin W. Benge, PhD
Provost & Professor in Church History
Union School of Theology, Bridgend, Wales

Book review editors: Josiah Michael Claassen, PhD cand.
The Southern Baptist Theological Seminary, Louisville, Kentucky
jclaassen800@students.sbts.edu

C. Anthony Neel, PhD cand.
The Southern Baptist Theological Seminary, Louisville, Kentucky
cneel914@students.sbts.edu

Editorial board
Cindy Aalders, DPhil
Director of the John Richard Allison Library
Assistant Professor of the History of Christianity
Regent College, Vancouver

Ian Hugh Clary, PhD
Assistant Professor of Historical Theology
Colorado Christian University, Lakewood, Colorado

Dustin W. Benge, PhD
Provost & Professor in Church History
Union School of Theology, Bridgend, Wales

Dustin B. Bruce, PhD
Dean & Assistant Professor of Christian Theology and Church History
Boyce College, Louisville, Kentucky

Chris W. Crocker, PhD
Pastor, Markdale Baptist Church, ON
Associate Professor of Church History,
Toronto Baptist Seminary, Ontario

Chris Chun, PhD
Professor of Church History & Director of the *Jonathan Edwards Center*
Gateway Seminary, Ontario, California

Jenny-Lyn de Klerk, PhD
Puritan Project Assistant
Regent College, Vancouver

Jason G. Duesing, PhD
Provost & Professor of Historical Theology
Midwestern Baptist Theological Seminary, Kansas City, Missouri

Nathan A. Finn, PhD
Provost & Dean of the University Faculty
North Greenville University, Tigerville, South Carolina

C. Ryan Griffith, PhD
Independent Scholar
Minneapolis, Minnesota

Peter Morden, PhD
Senior Pastor/Team Leader, Cornerstone Baptist Church
Leeds, England
& Distinguished Visiting Scholar
Spurgeon's College, London

Adriaan C. Neele, PhD
Director, Doctoral Program
& Professor of Historical Theology
Puritan Reformed Theological Seminary, Grand Rapids, Michigan
& Research Scholar
Yale University, Jonathan Edwards Center, New Haven, Connecticut

Tom Nettles, PhD
Emeritus Professor of Church History
The Southern Baptist Theological Seminary, Louisville, Kentucky

Robert Strivens, PhD
Pastor, Bradford on Avon Baptist Church (UK)
& Lecturer in Church History, London Seminary

S. Blair Waddell, PhD
Pastor, Providence Baptist Church, Huntsville, Alabama

Contents

The Journal of Andrew Fuller Studies
No. 3, September 2021

Editorial Michael A.G. Haykin	9
Articles The union of doxology and theology: A comparative study of Jonathan Edwards and Anne Duton Holly M. Farrow	11
The preacher and his sermon: Andrew Fuller's reading of Jean Claude Steele B. Wright	35
Andrew Fuller's preaching on the Psalms Nicholas J. Abraham	49
Thomas Scott and the Baptists Timothy Warren Scott	69
Texts & documents "Faithful and disinterested friendship": A letter of James Hinton ed. Chance Faulkner	83
"…With politics I never meddle, though my heart cannot be indifferent to the happiness of man": A letter of James Hinton on religious liberty ed. Chance Faulkner	87
A letter of Thomas Davis on his conversion ed. Michael A.G. Haykin	91
Book reviews	95
Short notices	107

Editorial

Michael A.G. Haykin

Michael A.G. Haykin is Chair and Professor of Church History and Director, The Andrew Fuller Center for Baptist Studies at The Southern Baptist Theological Seminary, Louisville, Kentucky.

A few years after the devastation of World War I, W.T. Whitley (1861–1947), one of the pioneers of the modern study of Baptist history, published a magisterial work, *A History of British Baptists*. It set a new standard for the study of its subject, though a major flaw of the book is that Whitley tends to dismiss the importance of theological reflection in Baptist history. And certain figures, like Anne Dutton, come in for fairly rough treatment. Whitley describes Dutton as a "censorious spirit" who "aspired to be the Countess of Huntingdon of the [Baptist] denomination." Rather than pouring out a flood of pamphlets, many of them deemed by Whitley to be unduly critical and hindrances to the advance of the Baptist cause, the Baptist historian suggested that she would have done better to have gotten up on her horse and like Whitefield or Wesley, become an itinerant evangelist![1] Thankfully, recent scholarship is increasingly cognizant that Dutton's extensive corpus is a treasure-trove of spirituality and theological reflection. Holly Farrow's comparative study of Dutton and her more famous contemporary, Jonathan Edwards, the American Augustine, builds on this new perspective on Dutton.

In similar fashion, there is growing recognition that Andrew Fuller is one of the great pastor-theologians of the eighteenth century (an affirmation befitting

---

[1] W.T. Whitley, *A History of British Baptists* (London: Charles Griffin & Company, Ltd., 1923), 214–215. As Ian Sellers notes of this work: "The *History* reveals that its author was uninterested in and rather suspicious of theological enterprise. His impatience is marked, not just with the High Calvinists, Gill and Brine, but with men such as Isaac Watts and Robert Robinson who spent time on the academic problem of the Person of Christ rather than on converting England" ("W.T. Whitley: A Commemorative Essay," *The Baptist Quarterly* 37, no.4 [October 1997]: 166).

this journal!). The other two articles in this issue both explore one element of Fuller's legacy: the pastoral ministry of Fuller in the pulpit. And both essays break new ground. Steele Wright looks at the influence of a famous essay on preaching by the Huguenot Jean Claude on Fuller's sermon preparation while Nicholas Abraham examines Fuller's preaching on one of Fuller's favourite portions of the Word of God, the Psalter.

For me, Abraham's essay brings to mind a pressing need for Baptist scholarship, namely, the detailed examination of how Baptist have interpreted both whole books and individual texts of the Scriptures. There has been study galore of how Baptists have viewed the Bible as inspired and infallible and utterly authoritative. But my question is: how exactly have Baptist read the Word of God and why? Hopefully, future issues of this journal can play a rôle in answering that question.

Our final article in this issue is a celebration of the catholicity of Thomas Scott and his friendships with a number of Baptist leaders, including Andrew Fuller. In this bicentennial year of Thomas Scott's homegoing to glory, author Timothy Scott (no relation to the eighteenth-century Bible commentator) rightly believes that he ought to be remembered for these, and other, important Christian virtues. Reading this essay, I saw Scott's life as a great rebuke to far too many Christians of our day who have been involved in bitter divisions over what can only be regarded as tertiary issues. We need to pray that many of Scott's temper and mindset will be raised up in these challenging times.

The union of doxology and theology: A comparative study of Jonathan Edwards and Anne Dutton"[1]

Holly M. Farrow

Holly M. Farrow is a PhD candidate in Church Music and Worship at Southwestern Baptist Theological Seminary.

> "And safely bring them home again, through all these various ways,
> Infinite wisdom did ordain electing love to praise."
> (Anne Dutton, Hymn XVII)[2]

The simultaneous existence of the Age of Reason and the Age of Piety during the eighteenth century stands as a great historical paradox. Although it was an age marked by distinct inclinations toward science, logic, and human reasoning, the era also witnessed theologians and authors whose works expressed heightened levels of reverence, devotion, and religious experience. This study will provide a doctrinal and literary interaction between two such authors: Reformed pastor and revivalist Jonathan Edwards (1703–1758), who provided one of America's most prolific and impactful theological legacies, and Anne Dutton (1692–1765), a British Particular Baptist and pastor's wife who voiced a lifelong mission to point others to Christ through her extensive theological

---

[1] This essay was originally published in *Artistic Theologian* 8 (2020) and is reproduced here by permission.

[2] Anne Dutton, *Hymns Composed on Several Subjects* in her *A Narration of the Wonders of Grace* in, *Selected Spiritual Writings of Anne Dutton: Eighteenth Century, British Baptist, Woman Theologian*, ed. Joann Ford Watson, 7 volumes (Macon, GA: Mercer University Press, 2004), 2:192–193. Subsequent references to these volumes will be rendered thus *Selected Spiritual Writings of Anne Dutton*, ed. Watson, with the appropriate volume and page numbers.

writings in the form of treatises, poetry, hymns, and personal letters.³

A comparative study of the two theologians will offer a new perspective on spiritual writings during the Evangelical Revival and a new way to contemplate Edwards, especially since Anne Dutton is under-researched.⁴ Like Edwards, Dutton faithfully proclaimed a staunch defense of Calvinism against various Arminian doctrines that she deemed objectionable and "nurtured the distant American awakening" through her vocation of religious writing.⁵ As will be seen, for an eighteenth-century Baptist female author to have published works with a theological depth and acumen that could withstand a comparison to Edwards was remarkable and extraordinarily rare. Accordingly, the establishment of specific connections and correlations between Edwards and Dutton would be a useful and compelling addition to eighteenth-century evangelical research.

In this article, I will argue that Jonathan Edwards and Anne Dutton display a notable similarity of content, depth, and intensity, both in their doctrinal writings of theology and in their devotional language of doxology.⁶ To sustain this argument, I will first establish the historical context for the study by briefly noting the impact of Edwards upon Particular Baptists in England as well as Anne Dutton's position and influence during the eighteenth century. Next, after a brief discussion of the Puritanical notion of the joining of theology and doxology, I will compare specific theological works of Edwards and Dutton to elucidate striking resemblances in depth and content as demonstrated in their writings on such topics as *resignatio ad infernum*, union with Christ, justification by faith alone, and the Lord's Supper. As will be shown, both Edwards and Dutton shared the conviction that the Holy Spirit should receive equal

---

³ In a tirelessly devoted manner (much like that of Edwards), Dutton spent the greatest majority of her time writing, often upwards of sixteen hours per day. Dutton was so dedicated to her ministry of writing that she even expressed regret over the time spent eating and sleeping. See Joann Ford Watson, "Introduction" in her ed., *Selected Spiritual Writings of Anne Dutton*, 1:xxxvi.

⁴ See Michael Sciretti, "'Feed My Lambs': The Spiritual Direction Ministry of Calvinistic British Baptist Anne Dutton During the Early Years of the Evangelical Revival" (PhD dissertation, Baylor University, 2009), 8. Sciretti reports that even with the vast abundance of her extant theological discourses, "no critical evaluation of Dutton exists."

⁵ Barbara J. MacHaffie, *Her Story: Women in Christian Tradition* (Philadelphia, PA: Fortress Press, 1986), 84.

⁶ Throughout this project, the term "doxology" will refer to "vertical" language and expressions that either praise God or address him directly. For additional background on this definition, see Stuart Sheehan, "The Changing Theological Functions of Corporate Worship Among Southern Baptists: What They Were and What They Became (1638–2008)" (PhD dissertation, University of Aberdeen, 2017).

consideration and emphasis along with the Father and the Son in theological discourse.

In the next section of the article, I will identify several metaphors and figures of speech common to the writings of Edwards and Dutton (such as light, sweetness, and love), and will indicate similarity of usage. This section will also indicate the authors' mutual love for the Song of Solomon, whose rich imagery and symbolism made it a favorite book of both writers.

Finally, I will examine the intense doxological expression shared by Edwards and Dutton—a devotional use of language describing religious experiences that some scholars interpret as "mystical." Fredrick Youngs identifies several attributes of mystical religious experiences: impassioned feelings of bliss and peace, a strong awareness of the sacred, and an overwhelming sense of the presence and ineffability of God—perceptions that are indescribable and extend beyond the capacity of words.[7] Their shared use of rhapsodic language to express their experiences of the divine, along with the parallels of thought found within their theological treatises, will clearly indicate a remarkable, compelling likeness and connection between Edwards and Dutton.

The impact of Edwards and Dutton on Particular Baptists in England
During the eighteenth century, religious works by American authors were commonly and regularly read by British readers—particularly so among non-Anglican evangelicals. The works of Edwards were first received in England as a welcomed harbinger of revival. Additionally, David Bebbington asserts that Edwards held other points of interest for British believers: he was "a profound explorer of Christian doctrine" who captivated his readers' imaginations with his descriptions of revival and heightened Christian experiences.[8] Furthermore, he championed Calvinism in a manner that was "intellectually acceptable" and compatible with contemporary Enlightenment principles such as "light, liberty, and progress."[9] Most impactful of all (and of great significance to the present comparison to Dutton) was Edwards' "authority [in] *shaping theological discourse.*"[10]

Among British Particular Baptists, the writings of Jonathan Edwards were

---

[7] In this paper, the term "mystical" will refer only to these specifically named characteristics. See Fredrick Youngs, "Jonathan Edwards, a Mystic?," *Perspectives in Religious Studies* 38, no. 1 (Spring 2011): 52.

[8] David Bebbington, "The Legacy of Jonathan Edwards in Britain," in *The Global Edwards: Papers from the Jonathan Edwards Congress Held in Melbourne, August 2015*, ed. R.S. Bezzant (Eugene, OR: Wipf and Stock, 2015), 2–4.

[9] Bebbington, "The Legacy of Jonathan Edwards in Britain," 4.

[10] Bebbington, "The Legacy of Jonathan Edwards in Britain," 3. Emphasis added.

celebrated and his influence was profound and "decisive."[11] The *Faithful Narrative of Surprising Conversions* (first printed in London in 1737) was the first work of Edwards to impact England—it was widely read and received as "an exemplary narrative" that brought with it a "spirit of optimism and possibility."[12] Although originally a piece of personal communication between pastors, the *Narrative* was enthusiastically presented before entire congregations and appeared in various evangelical periodicals. In Hindmarsh's estimation, it was a "runaway best-seller" that invigorated the spiritual landscape of Britain and spurred on her believers to embrace the active work of evangelism. Succinctly put, the works of Edwards "gave them hope—hope that they might see revival, too."[13]

Although they were greatly encouraged by Edwards's dramatic accounts of revival in New England, the Particular Baptists still wrestled through various theological debates and controversies. Their emphasis on election and predestination caused some to espouse antinomianism, which maintained that because salvation comes "by grace and through faith alone"[14] and not by means of human effort, man's behavior was predestined and unbound by the obligations of moral law.[15] Because of a strongly emerging "hyper" Calvinism (a position held by a good number of influential theologians and pastors), many Calvinistic Baptists arrived at the conclusion that if certain people were not predestined for salvation, the matter was settled and no evangelical effort would change the outcome. With this outlook, offering the Gospel to the lost was "at best a waste of time, and at worst an insult to God and divine providence" and therefore to be avoided.[16]

The dilemma for the Particular Baptists was how to preach faith and repentance to all while remaining true to their Calvinist principles. In his *Freedom of the Will* (1754), Edwards provided Baptist preachers with the perfect answer:

---

[11] D. Bruce Hindmarsh, "The Reception of Jonathan Edwards By Early Evangelicals in England," in *Jonathan Edwards at Home and Abroad: Historical Memories, Cultural Movements, Global Horizons*, ed. David W. Kling (Columbia, SC: University of South Carolina Press, 2003), 207.

[12] Hindmarsh, "The Reception of Jonathan Edwards By Early Evangelicals in England," 203.

[13] Hindmarsh, "The Reception of Jonathan Edwards By Early Evangelicals in England," 202–203.

[14] See "Antinomianism" in *The Oxford Encyclopedia of the Bible and Ethics*, ed. James D.G. Dunn, *Oxford Biblical Studies Online*, http://www.oxfordbiblicalstudies.com/article/opr/t430/e10 (accessed November 17, 2019).

[15] Michael D. Thompson, "Edwards' Contribution to the Missionary Movement of Early Baptists" in *The Contribution of Jonathan Edwards to American Culture and Society: Essays on America's Spiritual Founding Father (The Northampton Tercentenary Celebration, 1703-2003*, ed. Richard A.S. Hall (Lewiston, NY: Edwin Mellen Press, 2008), 320.

[16] Thompson, "Edwards' Contribution to the Missionary Movement of Early Baptists," 320.

Mankind was endowed with the "natural ability" or potential to accept the Gospel. Even so, some individuals experience a "moral inability" to embrace salvation because of a steadfastness of sin springing from their own hearts.[17] Accordingly, it was clearly the "duty" or responsibility of each person to repent and come to faith. This realization—that a belief in the doctrine of election need not impede preaching repentance—enabled pastors to make an open invitation to all in good conscience. This newly found freedom and shift in doctrinal thinking greatly stimulated evangelism and missions among Particular Baptists.[18] Michael Watts observes that "the writings of the Congregational pastor of Northampton, Massachusetts led to religious revival among the Particular Baptists of Northamptonshire, England and set in train the dispersion of the principles of English Dissent to the four corners of the world."[19]

Within Anne Dutton's sphere of influence, her own extensive ministry of writing was securely set within this Particular Baptist theological context. Anne's husband, evangelical minister Benjamin Dutton (1691–1747), assumed the pastorate of the Particular Baptist church of Great Gransden in Huntingdonshire in 1732. Anne's distinguished ministry of writing began soon thereafter, appropriately coinciding with the early dawning of the Evangelical Revival.[20] By the year 1737, when Edwards' *Faithful Narrative of Surprising Conversions* first appeared in London, Anne had published seven discourses on various theological topics, including her acclaimed poetic work *Narrative on the Wonders of Grace* (1734) and *A Discourse upon Walking with God* (1735). By 1740, the full flames of revival were sweeping over England, and by August of 1741, Dutton's treatises were being published and circulated in *The Weekly History*. Scholars have recently acknowledged the full weight of Dutton's evangelical impact during this time, noting that she was "perhaps the most theologically capable and influential woman of her era, an uncommon interpreter of Scripture, and an obedient servant of Christ."[21]

In addition to her extensive theological publications, Dutton penned an immense number of personal letters of spiritual encouragement to evangelical leaders and lay people who sought her wisdom in both doctrinal and personal

---

[17] Thompson, "Edwards' Contribution to the Missionary Movement of Early Baptists," 322.

[18] Bebbington, "The Legacy of Jonathan Edwards in Britain," 6.

[19] Cited L.G. Champion, "Evangelical Calvinism and the Structures of Baptist Church Life," *The Baptist Quarterly* 28, no. 5 (January 1980): 197.

[20] Sciretti, "Feed My Lambs," 2. In this passage, Sciretti also notes the intriguing fact that Dutton's theological treatises and poetry were first published "two years before the conversion of George Whitefield and five years before the conversions of Charles and John Wesley."

[21] Karen O'Dell Bullock, "Anne Dutton" in *Handbook of Women Biblical Interpreters: A Historical and Biographical Guide*, ed. Marion Ann Taylor (Grand Rapids, MI: Baker Academic, 2012), 172–173.

matters of faith. Among her many correspondents were George Whitefield (1714–1770), John Wesley (1703–1791), Phillip Doddridge (1702–1751), Selina Hastings, Countess of Huntingdon (1707–1791), William Seward (1702–1740), and Howell Harris (1714–1773).[22] Dutton befriended Whitefield and fully supported his evangelical efforts at a time when most Calvinistic Baptists were distinctly "opposed to the new Evangelical movement."[23] William Seward, who accompanied Whitefield in his travels, expressed that Dutton's letters were "full of such comforts and direct answers to what I had been writing that it filled my eyes with tears of joy."[24] Welsh revivalist Howell Harris affirmed Dutton's ministry of writing when he confirmed to her that "our Lord has entrusted you with a Talent of writing for him."[25] In addition to these noteworthy friendships and associations, Dutton had a special concern for the newly converted who found themselves troubled in their personal circumstances or doubtful about whether they would be counted among God's elect. Dutton's influence eventually stretched across the Atlantic into the American colonies, where she gained a solid reputation particularly among converts in Georgia and South Carolina through her publications and personal correspondence.[26]

Whether Edwards and Dutton ever corresponded directly is unknown. Nevertheless, evidence that Dutton knew of Edwards and his writings does exist. In her Letter XX, Dutton mentions Edwards by name and comments at some length upon his "late account of the work of God in the conversion of souls to Christ in New England."[27] Moreover, because she was a published author and was particularly well-read (having frequently corresponded with several key evangelical ministers and having served as editor of the evangelical periodical *The Spiritual Magazine*), Dutton was engaged with contemporary evangelical writings and events throughout her life. In all probability, a figure of Edwards's magnitude would have impressed upon the shape and tone of Dutton's theological writings.

The theology of Edwards and Dutton: Expressions of resolute faith
To demonstrate the notable parallels of thought in the theological convictions

---

[22] Sciretti, "Feed My Lambs," 5. Additionally, through her published discourses, Dutton sparred theologically with John Wesley regarding his belief in the ability to attain a state of sinless perfection while on earth.

[23] Sciretti, "Feed My Lambs," 5.

[24] Stephen J. Stein, "A Note on Anne Dutton, Eighteenth-Century Evangelical," *Church History* 44, no. 4 (December 1975): 488.

[25] Stein, "A Note on Anne Dutton," 488.

[26] Stein, "A Note on Anne Dutton," 489.

[27] See Anne Dutton, Letter XX, in *Selected Spiritual Writings of Anne Dutton*, ed. Watson, 1:138–144.

of Edwards and Dutton, it is first important to note that the two theologians shared a common body of divinity handed down from their Puritan forefathers. "Communion with God," states J.I. Packer, is the nucleus of Puritan theology.[28] The firmly held beliefs of the Puritans led them to establish a faith system that was "first and foremost about the worship of God ... theology and the life informed by such convictions were to be one harmonious act" of worship and praise.[29] Put simply, worship is the "external manifestation" of theological "internal convictions."[30] Theology inspires doxology—and the two are intricately woven together and inseparable.

The theological legacy of the Puritans, inherited and expressed by Edwards and Dutton, was an unwavering commitment "to search the Scriptures, organize their findings, and then apply those to all areas of life."[31] Additionally, while the Puritans were exceptional interpreters of Scripture, "their intellectual rigor was matched or even surpassed by their piety."[32] Only through strict obedience and adherence to the Word, reflection upon God's character and his work among mankind, and the indwelling presence of the Holy Spirit could a believer properly live unto God, in harmony with his will and to his glory.[33] The Puritans also trusted that the influence of God would be visibly manifested within their practical, day-to-day life experiences. Succinctly put, their arduous intention was "to live *coram Deo*"—in the presence of God and "before the face of God."[34]

One of the "giants" among Puritan thinkers who undoubtedly impacted the theologies of Edwards and Dutton was John Owen (1616–1683). Timothy Edwards (1669–1758), Jonathan's father, owned a good number of Puritan classics in his library, including works by Owen—writings that are considered to also have been spiritually formative for his son.[35] In the case of Anne Dutton's works, the names of Puritan authors who influenced her writing are often cited,

---

[28] Cited Peter Beck, "Worshiping God with Our Minds: Theology as Doxology Among the Puritans," *Puritan Reformed Journal* 5, no. 2 (2013): 194.

[29] Beck, "Worshiping God with Our Minds," 194.

[30] Beck, "Worshiping God with Our Minds," 196.

[31] Joel R. Beeke, "Reading the Puritans," *Puritan Reformed Journal* 3, no. 2 (2011): 197.

[32] Beeke, "Reading the Puritans," 198.

[33] Beck, "Worshipping God with Our Minds," 196.

[34] Beeke, "Reading the Puritans," 199.

[35] Michael J. McClymond and Gerald R. McDermott, *The Theology of Jonathan Edwards* (New York, NY: Oxford University Press, 2012), 61.

and John Owen is among the men most frequently mentioned.[36]

The pathway to communion with God, in Owen's view, was a "proper biblical theology," achieved through careful exegesis that was precise and free of error.[37] As theological knowledge increases, communion with God deepens and matures. God's purposes in this communion are grounded in love and always to his greater glory: "God would have it so," writes Owen, "for the manifestation of his own glory. This is the first great end of all the works of God. That it is so is a fundamental principle of our religion. And how his works do glorify him is our duty to inquire."[38]

This notion is also found and clearly demonstrated in the writings of Edwards and Dutton. In his *Dissertation on the End for Which God Created the World* (1755), Edwards states that "the great and last end of God's works which is so variously expressed in Scripture, is indeed but *one*; and this *one* end is most properly and comprehensively called, the glory of God."[39] Similarly, in her treatise *A Discourse Upon Walking with God* (1735), Dutton writes that "God's end in walking with his People in Christ, and in all the Ways of Divine Appointment, is *ultimately his own Glory*; and subordinately their Good and Salvation."[40] As will be shown, the theological harmony and agreement shared by Edwards and Dutton extend to several additional religious topics that were points of discussion during the eighteenth century.

Resignatio ad infernum
The topic of *resignatio ad infernum* (resignation to hell) is a concept with a long history, having been discussed by theologians dating back to the medieval period. A person would voice a "willingness to be damned" if s/he had achieved such a selfless state of piety that if condemnation was ordained as part of the divine will, and if their damnation would somehow glorify God more than their salvation, it would gladly be accepted "out of absolute love and absolute obedience to God."[41] Edwards, however, considered this to be the mindset of a

---

[36] Sciretti, "Feed My Lambs," 119.

[37] Beck, "Worshiping God with Our Minds," 196.

[38] John Owen, *Christologia*, as quoted by Ryan L. Rippee, "John Owen On the Work of God the Father," *Puritan Reformed Journal* 8, no. 2 (2016): 90.

[39] Jonathan Edwards, *Dissertation on the End for Which God Created the World*, in *The Works of President Edwards* (New York, NY: Leavitt, Trow & Co., 1844), 2:254.

[40] Anne Dutton, *A Discourse Upon Walking with God*, in *Selected Spiritual Writings of Anne Dutton*, ed. Watson, 2:53. Emphasis added.

[41] Clark R. West, "The Deconstruction of Hell: A History of the Resignatio Ad Infernum Tradition" (PhD dissertation, Syracuse University, 2013), 4.

person who "seems" to have a love for God and Christ, but has "no grace." In a footnote written by Edwards in *Religious Affections*, he paraphrases a passage from his grandfather Solomon Stoddard's (1643–1729) *Guide to Christ*, stating that "sometimes natural men may have such violent pangs of false affection to God, that they may think themselves willing to be damned."[42] The concept appeared in Edwards's writing years earlier in the *Narrative of Surprising Conversions*; Edwards describes believers who have such a strong "sense of the excellency of God's justice" and an "exceeding loathing" of their own sinful unworthiness that they experience

> a kind of indignation against themselves, that they have sometimes almost called it a willingness to be damned; though it must be owned they had not clear and distinct ideas of damnation, nor does any word in the Bible require such self-denial as this. But the truth is, as some have more clearly expressed it, that salvation has appeared too good for them, that they were worthy of nothing but condemnation, and they could not tell how to think of salvation's being bestowed upon them, fearing it was inconsistent with the glory of God's majesty.[43]

Dutton addresses this matter in a personal letter to a man who was troubled that his love for God had not achieved "such a height" as to be content with damnation if it would "advance the Kingdom and the glory of Christ."[44] Dutton counsels that it had never once entered her mind that "God would be more glorified in my damnation than in my salvation."[45] In the next paragraphs of her letter, she expresses a view on the subject that is in complete agreement with that of Edwards:

> I think Mr. Edwards, in his late account of the work of God in the conversion of souls to Christ in New England, gives a hint concerning some persons who had such a sense of the justice of God in their damnation, if He were to send them to hell, that they were ready to express themselves after such a manner as if they were "content to be damned;" and then adds, "that he knows no Scripture that requires it." An absolute contentment with damnation is doubtless unlawful; it is incompatible with that

---

[42] Jonathan Edwards, *Religious Affections*, ed. John E. Smith, The Works of Jonathan Edwards, vol. 2 (New Haven, CT: Yale University Press, 2009), 147.

[43] Jonathan Edwards, *Narrative of Surprising Conversions*, in *The Works of President Edwards* (New York, NY: Robert Carter and Brothers, 1879), 3:247.

[44] Dutton, Letter XX, in *Selected Spiritual Writings of Anne Dutton*, ed. Watson, 1:138.

[45] Dutton, Letter XX, in *Selected Spiritual Writings of Anne Dutton*, ed. Watson, 1:138.

principle of self-preservation which God hath put into all His creatures.[46]

Dutton encourages the recipient of her letter to focus instead upon the eternal, "unsearchable" love of Christ, assuring him that the Father, to save his people from their sins, had placed "the cup of damnation, of curse and wrath, into Christ's hand, and through His drinking it up for us He puts the cup of salvation into ours."[47]

The believer's union with Christ through the Holy Spirit
Parallels of thought between Edwards and Dutton are also displayed through their corresponding points of view regarding union with Christ, a topic that both theologians wrote about extensively. Edwards states that "all divine communion, or communion of the creatures with God or with one another in God, seems to be by the Holy Ghost."[48] As Robert Caldwell aptly explains, "In the theology of Jonathan Edwards, the Holy Spirit's activity as the bond of the trinitarian union between the Father and the Son is paradigmatic for all other holy unions in his theology."[49] Edwards affirmed that the Spirit also creates the union between Christ's human and divine natures, the union that believers have with Christ, and the union that Christians have with each other.

In the view of Edwards, for a saint to have union with Christ requires an act of the indwelling Holy Spirit, who brings holy authority and influence into his life. Edwards clearly states that the Spirit

> unites himself with the mind of a saint, takes him for his temple, actuates and *influences* him as a new, supernatural principle of life and action… the Holy Spirit operates in the minds of the godly, by uniting himself to them, and living in them, and *exerting his own nature* in the exercise of their faculties.[50]

Dutton expresses the reality of divine influence upon the Christian believer in different words, yet the underlying message is essentially the same; the saint

---

[46] Dutton, Letter XX, in *Selected Spiritual Writings of Anne Dutton*, ed. Watson, 1:139.

[47] Dutton, Letter XX, in *Selected Spiritual Writings of Anne Dutton*, ed. Watson, 1:143.

[48] Edwards, "Miscellanies" No. 487, as discussed in Robert W. Caldwell III, *Communion in the Spirit: The Holy Spirit as the Bond of Union in the Theology of Jonathan Edwards* (Milton Keynes, UK: Paternoster, 2007), 86.

[49] Caldwell, *Communion in the Spirit*, 8.

[50] Edwards, "A Divine and Supernatural Light," in *The Works of President Edwards* (New York, NY: Robert Carter and Brothers, 1879), 4:440. Emphasis added. See also Caldwell, *Communion in the Spirit*, 102–104.

experiences union with Christ, whose influence enables him to live a new life:

> But that if any man be in Christ by *influential union*, if he be vitally *united to him as his root and head of influence*, he partakes of Christ's life, hath a sameness of nature with him, a new life of grace from Christ the new Adam communicated to him; or, that by virtue of his thus being in Christ, he (the man) is a new creature; old things are become new in him.[51]

The topic of union with Christ through the work of the Holy Spirit also appears in several of Dutton's hymns, such as the following example taken from Hymn L, "Faith, the Gift of God, the Effect of Christ's Death, and the Work of the Spirit," stanzas five and six. The biblical references provided for each line of poetry are Dutton's, and incidentally demonstrate a meticulous devotion to Scripture that is reminiscent of Edwards:

The Spirit works this grace,	1 Cor. xii.9.
By his almighty power,	Eph. i.19.
In every of the chosen race,	Acts xiii.48.
At the appointed hour.	John v.25.
Faith lives in Christ its root,	Gal. ii.20.
And 'cause its union lasts,	John xiv.19.
It brings forth all its precious fruit,	Col. i.6.
Though nipp'd with stormy blasts.[52]	1 Pet. i.6,7.

In sum, Edwards understood the Holy Spirit to be the "meeting place" of the communion shared by the Father and the Son—and consequently, the work of the Spirit forms the basis of all manifestations of Christian communion.[53] As such, Edwards firmly believed that the Holy Spirit should receive equal honor along with the Father and the Son; he perceived a notable "deficiency" in the church's discourse regarding pneumatology and sought to rectify it.[54] Anne Dutton shared Edwards's desire to give equal honor and consideration to the

---

[51] Anne Dutton, *A Postscript to A Letter lately published, on the Duty and Privilege of a Believer, to live by Faith, and to Improve his Faith unto Holiness*, in *Selected Spiritual Writings of Anne Dutton*, ed. Watson, 6:179. Emphasis added.

[52] Anne Dutton, *Hymns Composed on Several Subjects* in *A Narration of the Wonders of Grace*, in *Selected Spiritual Writings of Anne Dutton*, ed. Watson, 2:228.

[53] Caldwell, *Communion in the Spirit*, 45.

[54] Caldwell, *Communion in the Spirit*, 9.

Holy Spirit. In the Preface to *A Narration of the Wonders of Grace*, she writes:

> I would not have any from thence think, that I esteem that part of the Spirit's work as a wonder of grace *inferior* to the rest. No; I believe that all the acts and works of the three Persons in God, as they have a joint hand in the salvation of the elect, shine forth with as equal splendour.[55]

Justification
Another area of theological similarity between Edwards and Dutton comes to light when exploring their respective treatises regarding justification. Edwards's *Justification by Faith Alone* was published in 1738; Dutton's *A Treatise on Justification* was published anonymously two years later and went through three editions (1740, 1743, and 1778).

In his treatise, Edwards refutes the theological views of John Tillotson (1630–1694), a former Archbishop of Canterbury who believed that justification referred to the "pardon or remission of sins" and nothing more.[56] Edwards agreed that guilt and sin are indeed removed, but he also believed that an additional act takes place—the believer *gains* right standing before God through the imputation of the righteousness of Christ. Edwards wrote that "a person is said to be justified, when he is approved of God as free from the guilt of sin and its deserved punishment; and as having that righteousness belonging to him that entitles to the reward of life."[57] Edwards based his discourse on the following passage from Romans 4:5: "But to him that worketh not, but believeth on him that justifieth the ungodly, his faith is counted for righteousness," thereby confirming the traditional Reformed position that justification is by faith alone.

Edwards maintained that justification released believers from the bondage of sin and its rightful penalty and provides the gift of Christ's righteousness through imputation. The dual nature of justification correlates with the dual nature of Christ's sacrifice: his suffering erases the sinner's guilt, and his obedience provides "the reward of heaven."[58] Justification is based only on God's grace and not any "moral qualifications" of man. Here once again appears the concept of union with Christ, which occurs when the sinner accepts Christ's invitation to redemption. Edwards believed that spiritual union should be a

---

[55] Anne Dutton, *A Narration of the Wonders of Grace*, in *Selected Spiritual Writings of Anne Dutton*, ed. Watson, 2:114.

[56] Cited Michael McClenahan, "Justification by Faith Alone," in *A Readers Guide to the Major Writings of Jonathan Edwards*, ed. Nathan A. Finn and Jeremy M. Kimble (Wheaton, IL: Crossway, 2017), 84.

[57] Jonathan Edwards, "Justification by Faith Alone," in *The Works of President Edwards* (1879), 4:66.

[58] Sang Hyun Lee, "Grace and Justification by Faith Alone," in *The Princeton Companion to Jonathan Edwards*, ed. Sang Hyun Lee (Princeton, NJ: Princeton University Press, 2005), 137.

reciprocal "mutual act of both," in which each one receives and joins with the other.[59] Once a believer gains admission into communion with Christ, God sees the worthiness of Christ when looking upon the regenerate soul. Edwards teaches that the state of justification happens only by faith, the "instrument by which we receive Christ."[60]

Dutton's treatise on justification approaches the topic with a theological depth and sophistication that can withstand a comparison to Edwards; her acumen is lauded by the publisher of the 1778 edition, who stated that the treatise "needs no recommendation" because its content would "sufficiently recommend itself."[61] The treatise was thoroughly endorsed based on its skillful hermeneutic, described as "Scripture interpreting Scripture."[62] Dutton's heavy reliance upon the Bible is clearly seen in the detailed outline she provides for her discourse:

Section I. Of the Matter of Justification.
Jeremiah 23:6
This is the name whereby he shall be called,
THE LORD OUR RIGHTEOUSNESS.

Section II. Of the Manner of Justification.
Romans 4:6, 1:17, 10:10
God imputeth righteousness without works. The righteousness of God is revealed from faith to faith. With the heart of man believeth unto righteousness.

Section III. Of the Time of Justification.
Romans 4:25, 3:26, 1 Timothy 3:16
He was delivered for our offences, and raised again for our justification. God is just, and the justifier of him that believeth in Jesus. God was justified in the Spirit.

Section IV. Of the Effect of Justification.
Romans 5:1, 4:7, 2 Corinthians 5:14
Being justified, by faith we have peace with God, through our Lord Jesus Christ. Blessed are they whose iniquities are forgiven. The love of Christ,

---

[59] Lee, "Grace and Justification by Faith Alone," 138.

[60] Edwards, "Justification by Faith Alone," in *The Works of President Edwards* (1879), 4:68.

[61] Anne Dutton, *A Treatise on Justification*, in *Selected Spiritual Writings of Anne Dutton*, ed. Watson, 4:xiv.

[62] Dutton, *A Treatise on Justification*, in *Selected Spiritual Writings of Anne Dutton*, ed. Watson, 4:xv.

who died for us, constraineth us to live unto him.

Section V. An Objection, urged against the preceding Scripture-Doctrine of Justification, answered.
James 2:21
Was not Abraham our father justified by works, when he had offered his son Isaac upon the altar?

Section VI. The Insufficiency of legal obedience
to the justification of a Sinner.
Romans 3:20
By the deeds of the law, there shall no flesh be justified in his sight.

Section VII. The Conclusion.
Isaiah 45:24.
Surely, shall one say, In the Lord have I righteousness.[63]

A perusal of this outline shows the great extent and depth of Dutton's treatment of the subject, including the anticipation and explanation of possible objections, a feature also present in Edwards's treatise. Similarities to Edwards are also apparent in the themes and language she employs in explicating the topic: "the manner of justification, as with respect unto God, it is by imputation; and with respect to ourselves, by Faith."[64]

The Lord's Supper
Perhaps one of the strongest points of agreement shared mutually by Edwards and Dutton is their "highly sacramental" interpretation of the Lord's Supper. As Calvinists, both would have inherited the *via media* view of John Calvin (1509–1564). As Michael Haykin explains, the elements of the Table are "signs and guarantees of a present reality. To the one who eats the bread and drinks the wine with faith, there is conveyed what they symbolize, namely Christ. The channel, as it were, through which Christ is conveyed to the believer is none other than the Holy Spirit."[65] The Spirit connects or "links" believers to the risen Christ. In the supper, Christ is received "not because Christ inheres the elements, but because the Holy Spirit binds believers" to himself. If faith is not present, "only the bare elements are received."[66]

[63] Dutton, *A Treatise on Justification*, in *Selected Spiritual Writings of Anne Dutton*, ed. Watson, 4:67–146.

[64] Dutton, *A Treatise on Justification*, in *Selected Spiritual Writings of Anne Dutton*, ed. Watson, 4:95.

[65] Michael A.G. Haykin, *Eight Women of Faith* (Wheaton, IL: Crossway, 2016), 63.

[66] Haykin, *Eight Women of Faith*, 63.

Edwards maintained a strong conviction that one must be a professing Christian to gain admittance to the Table, reflecting his belief that there should be a "clear distinction between the church and the world" and that the Lord's Supper was a privilege reserved only for believers.[67] Defending his case with 1 Corinthians 11:28 ("Let a man examine himself, and so let him eat"), Edwards indicates that "it is necessary, that those who partake of the Lord's Supper, should judge themselves truly and cordially to accept of Christ, as their only Saviour and chief good; for of this the actions which communicants perform at the Lord's Table, are a solemn profession."[68]

Dutton's view of the supper had a historical foundation in the *Second London Confession of Faith* (1689), which ratified for Baptists that the ordinance serves as "confirmation of the faith of believers ... their spiritual nourishment, and growth in him."[69] Therefore, and not surprisingly, Dutton concurs with Edwards completely; in her treatise *Thoughts on the Lord's Supper* (1748), she states clearly that the Supper is only for the members of Christ's body, the Church: "For as the Lord's Supper is a Church-Ordinance, those that are the subjects thereof must be Church Members."[70]

For both Edwards and Dutton, the ordinance of the Lord's Supper demanded solemnity, reverence, and preparation of heart. Edwards expressed in no uncertain terms the "magnitude of the sacrament," warning that "those who contemptuously treat those symbols of the body of Christ slain and his blood shed, why, they make themselves guilty of the body and blood of the Lord, that is, of murdering him."[71] Dutton's words express the same conviction; she insists that anyone who partakes of the elements without receiving Christ by faith in their hearts is "so far from partaking of the Lord's Supper, that they are guilty of a great Abuse of it: Not discerning the Lord's Body therein, which can only be done by Faith, they become guilty of the Body and Blood of the Lord, 1 Cor.

---

[67] Jonathan Edwards, *A Humble Inquiry into the Rules of the Word of God Concerning the Qualifications Requisite to a Complete Standing and Full Communion in the Visible Christian Church*, as discussed in Mark E. Dever, "Believers Only—Jonathan Edwards and Communion," *Bibliotheca Sacra* 172 (July–September 2015): 262.

[68] Dever, "Believers Only," 262.

[69] Michael A. G. Haykin, "His Soul-Refreshing Presence: The Lord's Supper in Baptist Thought and Experience in the 'Long' Eighteenth Century" (Lecture, Institute for Christian Worship Lectures, The Southern Baptist Theological Seminary [February 2008]: 2).

[70] Anne Dutton, *Thoughts on the Lord's Supper: Relating to the Nature, Subjects, and Right Partaking of this Solemn Ordinance* (London: J. Hart, 1748), 9.

[71] Matthew Westerholm, "The 'Cream of Creation' and the 'Cream of Faith': The Lord's Supper as a Means of Assurance in Puritan Thought," *Puritan Reformed Journal* 1 (2011): 209.

11.27."[72] The weight of these strong words clearly indicate that both Edwards and Dutton believed the observance of the Lord's Supper to be an occasion that demanded the utmost solemnity, reverence, and piety.

Coming together by faith to the Lord's Table was also an endeavor of the soul to gain spiritual sight, to look upon Christ "with spiritual eyes."[73] This spiritual sight was not merely attaining intellectual insight into doctrine; it was an engagement or "betrothal" of the heart in which a "mixture of affections" was to be anticipated. Consequently, a believer could feel sorrow for his sins while simultaneously rejoicing in Christ's willingness to die in his place.[74] Edwards, in a sermon on Luke 22:19 preached in June of 1734, declared: "Another thing meant by "Do this in remembrance of Me" is that we should do it to revive suitable affection towards Christ, not merely to revive thoughts of Christ in our understanding, but also suitable exercises towards Him in our hearts."[75] Dutton similarly references affections within the Lord's Supper, and her message closely resembles that of Edwards: "We ought then, in an especial Manner … to regard the affections of our souls, that they intensely fix upon Christ crucified, that glorious object presented to our Faith, and act suitably towards him."[76]

In the view of Edwards and Dutton, when the elements of the Supper are received by faith, the Christian receives the body and blood of Christ spiritually, signifying union with him.[77] Around the years of 1750–1751, Edwards preached a sermon based on 1 Corinthians 10:17 in which he distinctly states that the Lord's Supper is "a representation of the union of Christ and His people, a union of hearts … here is also represented their union one with another, for here they meet together as brethren, as children of one family, as one spouse of Christ."[78] Dutton also employs language that speaks of union with Christ while feasting at his Table: "So by our repeated eating of Christ by Faith, in this Ordinance, our spiritual life is maintain'd and increased, we grow up into Union and Communion with Him."[79]

---

[72] Dutton, *Thoughts on the Lord's Supper*, 22–23.

[73] Westerholm, "The Cream of Creation," 210.

[74] Westerholm, "The Cream of Creation," 212.

[75] Jonathan Edwards, "The Lord's Supper Ought to Be Kept Up and Attended in Remembrance of Christ," in *Sermons on the Lord's Supper*, ed. Don Kistler (Orlando, FL: Northampton Press, 2007), 60.

[76] Dutton, *Thoughts on the Lord's Supper*, 56–57.

[77] Westerholm, "The Cream of Creation," 215.

[78] Jonathan Edwards, "The Lord's Supper Was Instituted as a Solemn Representation and Seal of the Holy and Spiritual Union Christ's People Have with Christ and One Another," in *Sermons on the Lord's Supper*, ed. Kistler, 74.

[79] Dutton, *Thoughts on the Lord's Supper*, 39.

Edwards and Dutton both viewed the ordinance as a "seal" of this union with Christ, presenting the Supper as "a foretaste of the marriage supper of the Lamb," an eschatological reality of the coming Kingdom of God.[80] Edwards, in a sermon based on Luke 14:16, implored his listeners to consider all the glorious provisions that God has made:

> Is it not worth the while to accept any invitation to come to the marriage supper of the Lamb? Blessed and happy are they who enter in with God into the marriage. Yea, is not she blessed who shall be the bride, the Lamb's wife, to whom it shall be granted to be clothed in fine linen, clean and white, which is the righteousness of the saints (Revelation 19:8).[81]

Dutton offers her readers a similar vision of the resplendent future awaiting those who are in Christ: "The Lamb will bring you as his Bride, into the Bride Chamber, and set you as married to the Lord, to feast with Him at his Marriage Supper."[82]

Finally, the similarities between Edwards and Dutton on the Lord's Supper can be traced even more closely, to specific wordings and phrasings. Edwards preached that "Christ was not only with His disciples at the first sacrament, but He *sits with His people* in every sacrament."[83] Dutton's view matches that of Edwards both in meaning and expression: "the King is pleas'd to *sit with us*, at his Table."[84] Additionally, Dutton and Edwards share a specific commonality of language in their descriptions of what is imparted to the saint during the Supper. "As our Lord is spiritually present in his own ordinance," Dutton writes, "so he therein and thereby doth actually communicate, or give himself, *his body broken, and his blood shed*, with *all the benefits* of his death, to the worthy receivers."[85] Correspondingly, in his *An Humble Inquiry*, Edwards writes that "Christ presents himself" through the sacrifice of his "*body broken and his blood shed*," to "impart to them *all the benefits* of his propitiation and salvation."[86]

---

[80] McClymond and McDermott, *The Theology of Jonathan Edwards*, 491–92.

[81] Edwards, "The Spiritual Blessings of the Gospel are Fitly Represented by a Feast," in *Sermons on the Lord's Supper*, 125.

[82] Dutton, *Thoughts on the Lord's Supper*, 36.

[83] Edwards, "The Spiritual Blessings of the Gospel are Fitly Represented by a Feast," in *Sermons on the Lord's Supper*, ed. Kistler, 123. Emphasis added.

[84] Haykin, "His Soul-Refreshing Presence," 3. Emphasis added.

[85] Haykin, "His Soul-Refreshing Presence," 3. Emphasis added.

[86] Emphasis added. See discussion of this passage in Caldwell, *Communion in the Spirit*, 161–165.

As has been shown, the kinship and correlations found in the respective theological expressions of Edwards and Dutton are extensive. After having established the numerous parallels of thought found in their doctrinal writings, I now turn my attention to their doxological language of praise.

The doxology of Edwards and Dutton: voices in harmony

The Puritans saw their Creator as Lord over each aspect of human life—therefore human behavior must be governed by a proper understanding of God. A proper theology did not consist of merely a "set of rules" but was an all-consuming, authoritative "life-force."[87] Beck explains: "Biblical theology produces practical results and eternal praise."[88] And according to the seventeenth-century Puritan John Owen, "the vital force of theology is piety, it is worship."[89] Dutton alluded to this truth herself when she penned the words, "Salvation and Glory are put together in the Doxologies of the saved ones."[90] As will be seen in the next sections, a harmonious synthesis and union of theology and doxology are demonstrated in the highly expressive language of Edwards and Dutton.

Metaphoric language common to Edwards and Dutton: Types and tropes

Edwards states that "types are a certain sort of language, as it were, in which God is wont to speak to us."[91] Figures or types in the Old Testament foreshadow subjects and occasions found in the New Testament. In his *Images of Divine Things* notebook of 1728, Edwards speaks of types that depict "the way all things point beyond themselves" to demonstrate a "higher spiritual principle."[92] For example, Edwards states that "the rising and setting of the sun is a type of the death and resurrection of Christ" and that "the juice of the grape is a type of the blood of Christ."[93] Dutton also references the use of types in her writing; in her *Discourse Upon Walking with God*, she states: "As a Type of Christ, Joseph

---

[87] Beck, "Worshiping God with Our Minds," 203.

[88] Beck, "Worshiping God with Our Minds," 198.

[89] Beck, "Worshiping God with Our Minds," 197.

[90] Dutton, *A Discourse Upon Walking with God*, in *Selected Spiritual Writings of Anne Dutton*, ed. Watson, 2:57.

[91] Quoted by Tibor Fabiny, "Edwards and Biblical Typology," in *Understanding Jonathan Edwards: An Introduction to America's Theologian*, ed. Gerald R. McDermott (New York, NY: Oxford University Press, 2009), 99.

[92] Jennifer L. Leader, "In Love with the Image: Transitive Being and Typological Desire in Jonathan Edwards," *Early American Literature* 41, no. 2 (2006): 157.

[93] Jonathan Edwards, *Images or Shadows of Divine Things*, ed. Perry Miller (Westport, CT: Greenwood Press Publishers, 1948), 58 and 68.

had this Name of *the Shepherd of Israel* given him, Gen. 49.24."[94] The concept of types even appears in Dutton's hymnody:

The law had figures, types and shades,	Heb. ix.9.
Of glorious things to come;	Chap. x.1.
Which in the gospel are display'd	Col. ii.17.
And follow in their room.[95]	

This sophisticated use of typological language by Edwards and Dutton points their readers to "an iconic window" through which they may "catch a glimpse of the desired eternal."[96]

Tropes: Light
The way to come to know Edwards best, in the estimation of Ronald Story, is "chiefly through his language."[97] Story concurs with Marsden, who stated that the central core of Edwards's life was "his devotion to God expressed with pen and ink."[98] Story identifies several frequently recurring "tropes" or metaphorical figures of speech found in the works of Edwards; after identifying them, I will then demonstrate their usage in the works of Dutton.

First and foremost, "light was Edwards's favorite image and metaphor," observes Story, because Scripture hallows the concept of light from the very dawning of Creation through the coming of Christ, the Light of the World.[99] God is the "Father of Lights" and the saints walk together in the light of Christ, as "children of light."[100] The most significant symbolism associated with Edwards's treatment of light is that it represents "the beams of God's glory," his holiness, and the "manifestation of the excellency" of God, who is the Light to all creation in the same way the "fullness of the sun" touches, illumines, and brings warmth to all in the natural world. In his *Covenant of Redemption*, Edwards

---

[94] Dutton, *A Discourse Upon Walking with God*, in *Selected Spiritual Writings of Anne Dutton*, ed. Watson, 2:68.

[95] Anne Dutton, Hymn III, "The Glory of the Gospel Above the Law," in her *Hymns Composed on Several Subjects*, in *A Narration of the Wonders of Grace* in *Selected Spiritual Writings of Anne Dutton*, ed. Watson, 2:178.

[96] Leader, "In Love with the Image," 167.

[97] Ronald Story, *Jonathan Edwards and the Gospel of Love* (Amherst, MA: University of Massachusetts Press, 2012), 28.

[98] Story, *Jonathan Edwards and the Gospel of Love*, 28.

[99] Story, *Jonathan Edwards and the Gospel of Love*, 28.

[100] Story, *Jonathan Edwards and the Gospel of Love*, 29.

writes, "That beauteous light with which the world is filled in a clear day, is a lively shadow of His spotless holiness."[101] Dutton speaks of light in much the same manner as Edwards; in her treatise, *A Discourse Upon Walking with God* (1735), she writes: "God is Light; Light here, as I conceive, is put for Holiness. And we may read it thus, God is *Holiness*, and in him is no darkness, no sin … And if we thus walk in the Light, as he is in the Light, we have Fellowship one with another. God with us, and we with God."[102] The metaphor of light as the brightness of Christ also occurs in Dutton's hymnody:

No wonder that the moon and stars	Heb. viii.13.
Are vanish'd out of sight;	
Since Christ, the glory-sun appears	Chap. ix.11.
With his out-shining light.[103]	

Sweetness

Another figure of speech used by both Edwards and Dutton is the word "sweet," described by Story as one of the most prevalent descriptive words "in the Edwardsian lexicon."[104] Edwards uses the figure of sweetness to make declarative assertions about "God, grace, and the community of Christians."[105] Edwards describes the beauty of Christ as "most sweet" and rejoices in "sweetly conversing" with him. The Song of Solomon "sweetly sings" about the eternal marriage feast of Christ and the Church. The Persons of the Trinity share among themselves an "infinitely sweet energy which we call delight."[106] When writing about conversion, Edwards declared that it is a sweetness understood only by those who have tasted it. Those who embrace true religion experience the beauty of Christ, which exceeds the vain pleasures of this world "as much as gold and pearls" exceed "dirt and dung."[107] In the works of Dutton, the concept of sweetness regularly finds expression when speaking of the communion between God

---

[101] Quoted by Paul R. Baumgartner in "Jonathan Edwards: The Theory Behind His Use of Figurative Language," *Publications of the Modern language Association* 78, no. 4 (September 1963): 322.

[102] Dutton, *A Discourse Upon Walking with God*, in *Selected Spiritual Writings of Anne Dutton*, ed. Watson, 2:21.

[103] Dutton, Hymn III, "The Glory of the Gospel Above the Law," in *Selected Spiritual Writings of Anne Dutton*, ed. Watson, 2:178.

[104] Story, *Jonathan Edwards and the Gospel of Love*, 45.

[105] Story, *Jonathan Edwards and the Gospel of Love*, 45.

[106] Story, *Jonathan Edwards and the Gospel of Love*, 45–46.

[107] Story, *Jonathan Edwards and the Gospel of Love*, 47. In his discussion of these passages, Story cites Yale edition of *The Works of Jonathan Edwards*, 19:82–85.

and his people: "In the Way of Faith, or divine Revelation, they sweetly walk and talk together as Friends … in the Way of instituted Worship, God and his People sweetly commune together."[108] In her hymnody, Dutton expresses the sweetness of salvation:

> Salvation, O how sweet,   Ps. lxxxix.15.
> How joyful is the sound!
> Free reigning grace, through Jesus Christ,   Rom. v.21.
> O how it doth abound.[109]   Verse 20.

Edwards's and Dutton's "mystical" language and experience: Divine love
The intense spiritual experiences recorded by Edwards and Dutton are often described as "mystical" because they express an overwhelming desire "to be united in rapturous love with [their] Creator."[110] Edwards stated that "true religion is summarily comprehended in love" and ultimately, all things unite and "resolve into love."[111] Frequently in his writings on divine love, Edwards uses wordings and metaphoric language that possess a "lyrical, near-mystical" quality because he writes of a holy love that infinitely extends into all eternity. Succinctly put, love—in all its forms—points the elect to the future eschatological reality of Heaven. Edwards employs "soaring, ecstatic language" to depict the heavenly kingdom as a place where love is perfectly united and realized between God and all its citizens: "The very light which shines in and fills that world is the light of love. It is beams of love; for it is the shining of the glory of the Lamb of God, that most wonderful influence of lamblike meekness and love which fill the Heavenly Jerusalem with light."[112]

Passages from Edwards's *Personal Narrative* clearly display a heightened or "mystical" sense of language and expression:

> And as I was walking there, and looked up on the sky and clouds; there came into my mind, a sweet sense of the glorious majesty and grace of God, that I know not how to express. I seemed to see them both in a sweet conjunction: majesty and meekness joined together … there seemed to

---

[108] Dutton, *A Discourse Upon Walking with God*, in *Selected Spiritual Writings of Anne Dutton*, ed. Watson, 2:44–45.

[109] Anne Dutton, Hymn XXXVI, "Salvation in Election, and Covenant Settlements," in her *Hymns Composed on Several Subjects*, in *A Narration of the Wonders of Grace* in *Selected Spiritual Writings of Anne Dutton*, ed. Watson, 2:212.

[110] Youngs, "Jonathan Edwards, A Mystic?," 49.

[111] Story, *Jonathan Edwards and the Gospel of Love*, 99 and 102.

[112] As quoted by Story, *Jonathan Edwards and the Gospel of Love*, 121.

be, as it were, a calm, sweet cast, or appearance of divine glory, in almost everything. God's excellency, his wisdom, his purity, and love seemed to appear in everything; in the sun, moon, and stars; in the clouds, and blue sky; in the grass, flowers, trees; in the water and all nature.[113]

Elsewhere in his conversion narrative, Edwards reported that he felt an overwhelming "sense of the glory of the divine being" and pondered how happy he would be if he "might enjoy that God, and be wrapt up to God in heaven."[114] He also described feeling "an inward sweetness" that would "carry me away in my contemplations," kindling "a sweet burning in my heart."[115]

The conversion narrative of Anne Dutton displays a passion and energy quite similar to that of Edwards. She used intense language and imagery in her description of coming to Christ, declaring that she laid "prostrate before the throne of God's grace 'with a Rope about my Neck.'" Her expression was both plaintive and theological all at once: "Out of the Depths of Misery, I cry'd unto the Depths of Mercy."[116] After this experience, Dutton sought God "in the means of grace" through hearing sermons in corporate worship and reading the Bible. She describes her attainment of spiritual sight, in which she gained a vision of "such a ravishing Beauty, and transcendent Excellency in Christ that my Soul was ready to faint away with Desires after him."[117] Hindmarsh notes the "strikingly Edwardsian vision of the incandescent beauty" offered in Dutton's account.[118]

Like Edwards, Dutton often used language and imagery of love as found in the Song of Solomon, exclaiming that she was "pained with Love-Desires" and languished in "Love-sickness."[119] Additionally, doxological exclamations often appear within Dutton's theological treatises; for example, in *Thoughts on the Lord's Supper*, as she counsels the faithful regarding the proper, introspective manner in which to receive the Supper, Dutton suddenly erupts into rapturous praise:

---

[113] See this discussion in Youngs, "Jonathan Edwards, a Mystic?," 50.

[114] Youngs, "Jonathan Edwards, a Mystic?," 53.

[115] Youngs, "Jonathan Edwards, a Mystic?," 53.

[116] See D. Bruce Hindmarsh, *The Evangelical Conversion Narrative: Spiritual Autobiography in Early Modern England* (Oxford: Oxford University Press, 2005), 296.

[117] Hindmarsh, *Evangelical Conversion Narrative*, 296.

[118] Hindmarsh, *Evangelical Conversion Narrative*, 296.

[119] Hindmarsh, *Evangelical Conversion Narrative*, 299.

O what a Love, to our loving, lovely, dying, rising, reigning, coming Lord, doth his Love of Bounty, call for as Duty from us! Let us, attracted, allured, enkindled by the Power of infinite Love, cast our little Drop, into Love's vast Ocean, our little shining Spark, into Love's vehement Flame, into Love's adorable Brightness![120]

This type of emotive, rhapsodic language prompts Hindmarsh to make the following comparison: "If Catherine of Siena was a Third Order Dominican, then Anne Dutton must be reckoned something of a Third Order Baptist mystic."[121] Michael Sciretti concurs, stating that Dutton's language mirrors that of Christian mystics who went before her and that her theology was admirable because it is tempered with "the words and images of Scripture."[122]

Conclusion

This historical comparison of Edwards and Dutton affirms that evangelical communities in England and the American colonies exerted influence over one another and often shared a unity of thought that crossed denominational boundaries. Accordingly, scholars such as Richard Carwardine attest that the impact of revivalism upon the overall "shaping of society and culture" cannot be overstated.[123]

Through a close examination of their writings, I have shown in this study that Jonathan Edwards and Anne Dutton share a remarkable like-mindedness and a distinct resemblance in the content, depth, and intensity of their theological works and their doxological expressions of praise. I have shown the influence of Edwards within the historical context of the Particular Baptists, in which Anne Dutton performed an extraordinary ministry of religious writing during the Evangelical Revival. To elucidate their strikingly similar theology, I have provided a detailed analysis of their works on such topics as union with Christ, justification by faith alone, and the Lord's Supper. To illuminate the kinship of their doxology, I have identified figures of speech shared between the two authors and have demonstrated a mutual use of rapturous, ecstatic language to express their experiences of the divine.

In addition to its historical significance, the implications of this study are also useful in the consideration of current worship practices. Allen P. Ross states that for corporate worship to effectively reach its full potential, the church must

---

[120] Dutton, *Thoughts on the Lord's Supper*, 28.

[121] Hindmarsh, *Evangelical Conversion Narrative*, 299.

[122] Michael Sciretti, "Anne Dutton as a Spiritual Director," in *Christian Reflection* (2009): 31.

[123] Richard Carwardine, *Transatlantic Revivalism: Popular Evangelism in Britain and America 1790–1865* (Carlisle, UK: Paternoster, 2007), xiii.

have a thorough understanding of the "biblical theology that informs worship."[124] As has been established, both Edwards and Dutton faithfully display an unswerving loyalty and commitment to the authority of Scripture—a rich theological legacy for present-day church leaders with like-minded commitments. Moreover, Inagrace Dietterich asserts that the proper "doing of theology—studying and talking about God—is the responsibility of all who participate in the church."[125]

Through their shared Puritanical lineage and their similar religious experiences, Jonathan Edwards and Anne Dutton knew that theology must be built upon a proper understanding of God and must encompass all of life. As a person contemplate the mysteries of God and begin to understand his glorious excellency, they are inspired to obedience and a visible amendment of life, which ultimately creates a desire to praise, worship, and glorify God. Right belief leads to right practice—theology becomes doxology.[126]

---

[124] Allen P. Ross, *Recalling the Hope of Glory: Biblical Worship from the Garden to the New Creation* (Grand Rapids, MI: Kregel Publications, 2006), 38.

[125] Inagrace T. Dietterich, "Sing to the Lord a New Song: Theology as Doxology," *Currents in Theology and Mission* 41, no. 1 (February 2014): 24.

[126] Beck, "Worshiping God with Our Minds," 201–203.

The preacher and his sermon: Andrew Fuller's reading of Jean Claude

Steele B. Wright

Steele B. Wright is a PhD student in Christian Preaching at The Southern Baptist Theological Seminary. His research is focused on the preaching of Andrew Fuller. Currently, Steele and his wife, Brooke, reside in Knoxville, Tennessee, where Steele serves as a Pastor at Lonsdale Community Church.

Andrew Fuller (1754–1815) was in the early years of his ministry at Soham Baptist Church when Robert Robinson (1735–1790) first published his translation of Jean Claude's famous *Essay on the Composition of a Sermon* in 1778–1779.[1] In the years following its publication, Claude's *Essay* exerted considerable influence throughout England and especially among the Particular Baptists. The argument of the present study is that Claude's *Essay* served as the primary homiletical guide for Fuller in his own preaching ministry. Along with Claude, Fuller counseled preachers to build their sermons upon a single text or doctrine, which they intended to explain, establish, and apply while maintaining clear language and a unified design. Though Fuller relied heavily on Claude's *Essay*, he nevertheless retained a distinctly evangelical flavor in his own instructions on preaching as he emphasized the need to preach Christ in every sermon and offer the gospel to the unconverted.

While others have noted the significance of Claude's *Essay* among Particular Baptists generally, and Fuller in specific, no study has read Claude's *Essay*

---

[1] The first volume of Robinson's translation was published in 1778 with the second volume appearing the following year. See Jean Claude, *An Essay on the Composition of a Sermon*, trans. Robert Robinson, 2 vols. (1778–1779 N.p., Arkose Press, 2015).

alongside Fuller's instructions on preaching and sought to compare the two.[2] Therefore, the primary texts under consideration are Robert Robinson's two volume translation of Claude's *Essay* and Fuller's "Thoughts on Preaching," located in volume one of his *Works*.[3] In the first section, attention is given to the historical context to establish the connection between Fuller and Claude. In the second section, Claude's *Essay* is examined alongside Fuller's "Thoughts on Preaching" under two key headings: "The Principal Ends of Preaching" and "The Composition of the Sermon."

Jean Claude and the English Pulpit
At the height of his ministry, Jean Claude (1619–1687) served as the pastor of one of the most influential Huguenot congregations in France: the Charenton Church in Paris.[4] As a renowned preacher, polemical author, and key Protestant leader, Claude relentlessly defended the cause of the Reformation against the looming Catholic threat.[5] When King Louis XIV (1638–1715) revoked the Edict of Nantes (1598) in October 1685—effectively sealing the fate of the Protestant cause—Claude was given twenty-four hours to leave the country. As a result, he spent the final two years of his life exiled in the Netherlands. Shortly after his death in 1687, Claude's son, Isaac (1653–1695), published his *Essay on the Composition of a Sermon* to serve as a manual for preachers. In many ways, Claude's *Essay* marked a shift in Protestant homiletics from a prolonged

---

[2] See Keith S. Grant, Andrew Fuller and the *Evangelical Renewal of Pastoral Theology, Studies in Baptist History and Thought* (Eugene, OR: Wipf and Stock, 2013), 79–85; Stephen R. Holmes and Jonathan Woods, "Andrew Fuller's Soham Farewell Sermons: Context and Text," *Baptist Quarterly* 51, no. 1 (2020): 2–16; Peter J. Morden, " 'Be reconciled to trying disciplines': Andrew Fuller's Pastorate at Soham, 1775–1782," *Journal of Andrew Fuller Studies* 1, no. 1 (2020): 31–45. In his work on preaching, Hughes Old laments the lack of attention he gave to Robinson's translation of Claude's *Essay*, given its influence among Baptists. See Hughes Oliphant Old, *The Reading and Preaching of the Scriptures in the Worship of the Christian Church* (Grand Rapids, MI; Cambridge, UK: William B. Eerdmans Publishing Co., 2007), 6:730.

[3] Andrew Fuller, "Thoughts on Preaching: Letters I-IV," in *The Complete Works of the Rev. Andrew Fuller*, ed. Joseph Belcher (1845, Harrisonburg, VA: Sprinkle Publications, 1988), 1:712–727.

[4] For information on the life of Claude, see Pierre Bayle, "Claude (John)," in *An Historical and Critical Dictionary* (London, 1710), 2:996–999; Abel Rotholf de la Deveze, *The Life and Death of Monsieur Claude, the Famous Minister of Charentaon in France.*, ed. Thomas Dring (London, 1688). For a more recent study, see J. Wesley White, "Jean Claude (1619–1687): Huguenot Pastor and Theologian," *Mid-America Journal of Theology* 19 (2008): 195–205.

[5] On Claude's preaching and influence, see Hughes Oliphant Old, *Reading and Preaching of the Scriptures in the Worship of the Christian Church* (Grand Rapids, MI; Cambridge, UK: William B. Eerdmans Publishing Co., 2002), 4:444–446; Edwin Charles Dargan, "Jean Claude (1619–1687)," in his *A History of Preaching* (Grand Rapids, MI: Baker Book House, 1954), 124–27; J. Denny Autrey, "Factors Influencing the Sermonic Structure of Jean Claude and His Influence on Homiletics" (PhD dissertation, Southwestern Baptist Theological Seminary, 2013).

exposition on a series of verses toward the unifying of the sermon around a central theme.[6]

Robinson introduced Claude's *Essay* to the English-speaking world while recovering from a sprained ankle in the summer of 1776.[7] Nearly two decades after its initial publication, *The Evangelical Magazine* commended Robinson's translation for having contributed "much towards the improvement of our pulpit discourses."[8] Nevertheless, the reviewer lamented Robinson's copious notes, which exceeded the length of Claude's actual *Essay*. Having evidently shared the magazine's displeasure, the Anglican minister, Charles Simeon (1759–1836), published his own much shorter edition of Claude's *Essay* in 1797.[9]

According to J.W. Morris (1763–1836), Fuller discovered Claude's *Essay* soon after he entered the ministry.[10] From that point forward, Fuller considered himself indebted to Claude for "any just ideas which he entertained upon the subject" and he regularly recommended his work to others.[11] In his own "Essay on the Composition of a Sermon" Fuller plainly expressed his appreciation for Claude's work, "those however who wish to pursue this inquiry, and to become acquainted with the different methods of constructing a discourse, will meet with ample information in 'Claude's Essay on the composition of a Sermon,' as well as from other publications of subordinate merit."[12][13] That Fuller's essay bore the same title as Claude's further illustrates the French preacher's influence upon his own thinking.

---

[6] Autry sees Claude's *Essay* as a link between the preferred method of the early Christian tradition and that of the modern era. See Autrey, "Factors Influencing the Sermonic Structure," v.

[7] Graham W. Hughes, *With Freedom Fired: The Story of Robert Robinson, Cambridge Nonconformist* (London: Carey Kingsgate Press Limited, 1955), 54.

[8] "Review of Religious Publications: Claude's Essay on the Composition of a Sermon. Formerly translated from the French by the Rev. Robert Robinson," *The Evangelical Magazine* 5 (1797): 169.

[9] The reviewer further comments that Simeon was "sensible of the great utility of the Essay" but he doubted its widespread use given Robinson's many, often unrelated, notes. In "Review of Religious Publications," 169.

[10] J.W. Morris, *Memoirs of the Life and Writings of the Rev. Andrew Fuller* (London: T. Hamilton, 1816), 69.

[11] Morris, *Memoirs*, 69.

[12] It is unclear what Fuller meant by "other publications of subordinate merit." The only source he cited explicitly in his instructions on preaching was Edwards' *Thirty-Three Sermons*. See Fuller, *Works*, 1:720.

[13] Andrew Fuller, "Essay on the Composition of a Sermon: or, Plain and Familiar Thoughts, Addressed to a Young Minister from his Pastor," in *The Preacher; or Sketches of Original Sermons, Chiefly Selected from the Manuscripts of Two Eminent Divines of the Last Century, For the Use of Lay Preachers and Young Ministers*, ed. anon (Philadelphia: J. Whetham, 1838), 25. This same essay is found in Fuller, *Works*, 1:717–723, although the reference to Claude is omitted.

The principal ends of preaching
Woven throughout the fabric of Claude's *Essay* is a clear vision for preaching that guides his practical instructions. Claude expressed this vision simply through what he termed "the principal ends" of preaching—to instruct, please, and affect the listeners.[14] As O.C. Edwards has observed, this preaching triad is not original to Claude, but its roots go back to the early church and the ancient rules of rhetoric.[15] With this context in mind, Claude first advised the preacher to instruct his listeners in the truth of the text. However, this instruction extended beyond simply explaining its meaning. "For preaching," according to Claude, "is not only intended to give the sense of scripture, but also of theology in general; and, in short, to explain the whole of religion."[16]

In his efforts to instruct people in the ways of God, the preacher should also seek to please them.[17] Again Claude counseled, "the preacher must not always labour to carry the people beyond themselves, nor to ravish them into extacies [sic]: but he must always satisfy them, and maintain in them an esteem and an eagerness for practical piety."[18] When the mind is pleased at the prospect of godliness, the heart is drawn toward it. As a result, the preacher's efforts to instruct and please lead him to his final aim—to affect. Only when the affections have been reached is his task complete. Claude aptly summarized the necessity of p reaching to accomplish each of these ends:

---

[14] Claude wrote, "A sermon should instruct, please, and affect; that is, it should always do these as much as possible." In Claude, *Essay*, 1:26. Later, in his discussion on the Exordium (Introduction), he states more clearly, "There are three principal ends, which a preacher should propose, to instruct, to please, and to affect." In Claude, *Essay*, 2:473.

[15] Specifically, Augustine (354–430) and Cicero (106–43BC), who both relied on Aristotle's (384–344 BC) *Rhetoric*. See O.C. Edwards Jr., *A History of Preaching* (Nashville, TN: Abingdon Press, 2004), 452–455. For a criticism of Augustine's use of Greco-Roman rhetoric in preaching, see Duane Litfin, *Paul's Theology of Preaching: The Apostle's Challenge to the Art of Persuasion in Ancient Corinth* (Downers Grove, IL: IVP Academic, 2015), 48–53.

[16] Claude, *Essay*, 1:5.

[17] The language of "pleasing the hearers" may strike some modern readers as strange. In today's context, preaching to please elicits thoughts of changing the message for the sake of acceptance. However, this is not how Claude, nor Robinson, understood this idea. Paul's words in 2 Cor 4:2 supply the necessary context for their use of the term 'to please', "But we have renounced disgraceful, underhanded ways. We refuse to practice cunning or to tamper with God's word, but by an open statement of the truth we would commend ourselves to everyone's conscience in the sight of God" (English Standard Version).

[18] Claude, *Essay*, 1:13. An illustration later made famous by Jonathan Edwards comes to mind here. On the difference between engaging in speculative knowledge and being satisfied by divine truth, Edwards writes, "He that has perceived the sweet taste of honey, knows much more about it, than he who has only looked upon and felt it." See Jonathan Edwards, *The Religious Affections*, ed. John E. Smith, *The Works of Jonathan Edwards*, vol. 2 (New Haven, CT: Yale University Press, 2009), 2:272.

> Everybody can read scripture with notes and comments to obtain simply the sense: but we cannot instruct, solve difficulties, unfold mysteries, penetrate into the ways of divine wisdom, establish truth, refute error, comfort, correct, and censure, fill the hearers with an admiration of the wonderful works and ways of God, inflame their souls with zeal, powerfully incline them to piety and holiness, which are the ends of preaching, unless we go farther than barely enabling them to understand scripture.[19]

When the treasures of scripture are exposed and the listeners perceive their infinite value, their affections are moved, and the aim of preaching is fulfilled.

In "Letter II" of his "Thoughts on Preaching," Fuller offered four reflections based on what he described as the "epitome of the gospel ministry" of the apostles.[20] Fuller's vision of preaching rises to the surface in his answer to the question, "What must every sermon do?" First, "every sermon should have an errand," or a singular purpose that will result in eternal salvation if it is obeyed.[21] For the unbeliever, the errand is a summons to repentance and faith, while for the believer, it is an exhortation to persevere in godliness. A sermon without an errand is anything but a Christian sermon. It is possible, Fuller supposed, to fill the preaching hour "without imparting any useful instruction, without commending myself to any man's conscience, and without winning, or even aiming to win, one soul to Christ."[22] But such an effort would prove fruitless. In this passing comment, Fuller echoed Claude's three principal ends—to instruct, please, and affect—while placing a unique emphasis on the evangelistic nature of the sermon.

In addition to preaching with an errand, every sermon should also "contain a portion of the doctrine of salvation by the death of Christ."[23] Though Christ is not the primary theme of every text, he must be present in every sermon.[24] It is the preacher's responsibility to demonstrate the relationship between the subject of his text and the doctrine of the cross. "The preaching of Christ" concluded Fuller, "will answer every end of preaching. This is the doctrine which

---

[19] Claude, *Essay*, 1:5.

[20] Fuller, "Thoughts on Preaching: Letter II. Sermons—Subject-Matter of Them," in *Works*, 1:715.

[21] Fuller, "Thoughts on Preaching: Letter II. Sermons—Subject-Matter of Them," in *Works*, 1:715.

[22] Fuller, "Thoughts on Preaching: Letter II. Sermons—Subject-Matter of Them," in *Works*, 1:716.

[23] Fuller, "Thoughts on Preaching: Letter II. Sermons—Subject-Matter of Them," in *Works*, 1:716.

[24] Elsewhere Fuller warns, "We need not follow those who drag in Christ on all occasions ... Still less need we see him prefigured by everything in which a heated imagination may trace a resemblance." Nevertheless, he continues, "the sacred scriptures are full of Christ, and uniformly lead to him." In Fuller, "Letters on Systematic Divinity: Letter VII. The Uniform Bearing of the Scriptures on the Person and Work of Christ," in *Works*, 1:702–703.

God owns to conversion, to the leading of awakened sinners to peace, and to the comfort of true Christians."[25] A simple survey of Fuller's writings reveals a sustained focus on Christ as the principal end of both the written and the preached word.[26]

Next, as he proclaims the gospel, the preacher "must not imitate the orator, whose attention is taken up with his performance, but rather the herald, whose object is to publish, or proclaim, good tidings."[27] Here, Fuller's third reflection resembles Claude's exhortation that the preacher be both simple and grave. His words, remarked Claude, "should not be proposed in scholastic style nor common guise, but seasoned with a sweet urbanity, accommodated to the capacities of the people, and adapted to the manners of good men."[28] Lost in his discourse, the orator speaks beyond his people or below them, while the herald proclaims his message with a singular focus that is unconcerned with trivial things. In a sermon to fellow ministers, Fuller echoed Claude's sentiments, "Though the pulpit is not a place for affected pomposity, neither is it the place for mean and low language."[29]

In his final reflection, Fuller paired the obligation of declaring the gospel with "earnest calls, and pressing invitations, to sinners to receive it, together with the most solemn warnings and threatenings to unbelievers who shall continue to reject it."[30] Fuller's arrival at this conclusion represents a profound shift from his earliest days in ministry. As a young preacher, he followed in the footsteps of his former pastor, the High Calvinist John Eve, who "had little or nothing to say to the unconverted."[31] In time, Fuller grew increasingly dissatisfied with this approach and introduced appeals to unbelievers midway

---

[25] Fuller, "Preaching Christ," in *Works*, 1:504

[26] For Fuller's specific instructions on Christ-centered interpretation and preaching, see Fuller, "Preaching Christ," in *Works*, 1:501–502; Fuller, "God's Approbation of our Labours Necessary to the Hope of Success," in *Works*, 1:190–191; Fuller, "Letters on Systematic Divinity: The Uniform Bearing of the Scriptures on the Person and Work of Christ," in *Works*: 1:702–704; Fuller, "Thoughts on Preaching: Sermons—Subject-Matter of Them," in *Works*, 1:714–717. For an example of Fuller's Christ-centered expositions, see Fuller, "*Expository Discourses on the Book of Genesis*," in *Works*, 3:1–200.

[27] Fuller, "Thoughts on Preaching: Letter II. Sermons—Subject-Matter of Them," in *Works*, 1:716.

[28] Claude, *Essay*, 2:14.

[29] Fuller, "Ministers should be concerned not to be Despised," in *Works*, 1:489.

[30] Fuller, "Thoughts on Preaching: Letter II. Sermons—Subject-Matter of Them," in *Works*, 1:717.

[31] A.G. Fuller, "Memoir," in The Complete Works of the Rev. Andrew Fuller, ed. Joseph Belcher (1845, Harrisonburg, VA: Sprinkle Publications, 1988), 1:2. Reflecting on the High Calvinism of his early years, Fuller wrote, "The effect of these views was, that I had very little to say to the unconverted, indeed nothing in a way of exhortation to things spiritually good, or certainly connected with salvation." In Fuller, "Memoir," in Works, 1:15.

through his pastorate in Soham.[32] From then on, he issued invitations for sinners to receive the gospel and counseled young ministers to use the free offer "as part of our weapons of warfare" knowing that it is "through God that they become mighty to the pulling down of strong holds."[33] With the publication of *The Gospel Worthy of All Acceptation* in 1785, Fuller's position on this matter was confirmed and the force of his argument reverberated throughout every corner of Particular Baptist life.[34]

Interestingly, Claude lamented the abuses of divine sovereignty in his own day through the preaching of those he called "insidious sophisters." According to Claude, such preachers concluded that "since the conversion of men is by the almighty power of God, it is needless to preach his word" and "that it is in vain to tell a sinner, it is his duty to turn to God, as without efficacious grace."[35] While Claude addressed the free offer of the gospel in a passing illustration, Fuller situated it in a place of prominence in his instructions, an indication that the controversy of his day warranted a special emphasis in his preaching.[36]

The composition of the sermon
With Fuller and Claude's principal ends established, attention will now be given to each of their specific instructions on the composition of the sermon. What follows is a general outline of how Fuller instructed young ministers to approach the process of sermon preparation. Though priority is given to Fuller's method, Claude's *Essay* will be read alongside Fuller's instructions to further reveal points of continuity between the two preachers.

Cultivate a "spiritual frame of mind"
When Fuller described the pulpit as "an awful place," he understood both the gravity and the priority of preaching in the life of the Christian minster.[37] Neither the pulpit nor the study should be entered without fear and trembling. For this reason, Fuller opened his instructions by reminding his readers, "that which greatly aids in the composition and delivery of a sermon is spirituality

---

[32] Peter J. Morden, *The Life and Thought of Andrew Fuller* (1754–1815), Studies in Evangelical History and Thought (Milton Keynes: Paternoster, 2015), 43.

[33] Fuller, "Thoughts on Preaching: Letter II. Sermons—Subject-Matter of Them," in *Works*, 1:717.

[34] For the wider impact of this work, see Peter J. Morden, "Baptist and Evangelical: Andrew Fuller and The Gospel Worthy of All Acceptation," *Bulletin of the Strict Baptist Historical Society* 38 (2011): 1–20.

[35] Claude, *Essay*, 2:153.

[36] For historical context, see Geoffrey F. Nuttall, "Northamptonshire and The Modern Question: A Turning-Point in Eighteenth-Century Dissent," *The Journal of Theological Studies* 16, no. 2 (1965): 101–123.

[37] Fuller, "Memoir," in *Works*, 1:25.

of mind … The first thing, therefore before we sit down to study, should be to draw near to God in prayer."[38] For Fuller, the preacher may make use of every human gift and talent available to him, but if he neglects to enter into "a spiritual frame of mind" he will never truly understand the scriptures.[39]

Fuller's initial instructions to draw near to God in prayer flow from both his theology of preaching and his doctrine of the scriptures. In his first letter on "Expounding the Scriptures," Fuller observed, "A humble sense of our own ignorance, and of our entire dependence upon God, has also a great influence on our coming at the true meaning of his word."[40] His warning is clear. The preacher should not approach the scriptures like a professor approaches a textbook, merely searching for something to say. Rather, he must do so as a student who depends on the Spirit of God to lead him into all truth. Fuller made explicit what is largely implied throughout Claude's *Essay*. Aside from Claude's remark that the preacher must not be "a novice in divinity," he afforded less attention to this preliminary step than to the ensuing areas.[41]

Gain a clear idea of the text's "genuine meaning"
Both Fuller and Claude approached the scriptures with the understanding that every text has an objective meaning which the author intended to communicate to his original audience and which the preacher must now labor to uncover for himself. When choosing a passage, the preacher must be careful not to distort the author's meaning, either by carrying his sermon text too far or cutting it too short. Here, Claude offered a simple word of advice, "when the complete sense of the sacred writer is taken, you may stop; for there are few texts in scripture, which do not afford matter sufficient for a sermon; and it is equally inconvenient to take too much text, or too little; both extremes must be avoided."[42] It should be noted that the sermon examples found in Claude's *Essay* are typically confined to a single verse, usually from a New Testament epistle. While fewer in his examples, Fuller's texts are similarly taken from a single verse, as are the large majority of his published sermons.[43]

---

[38] Fuller, "Thoughts on Preaching: Letter III. The Composition of a Sermon," in *Works*, 1:717–718.

[39] Fuller, "Thoughts on Preaching: Letter I. Expounding the Scriptures," in *Works*, 1:713.

[40] Fuller, "Thoughts on Preaching: Letter I. Expounding the Scriptures," in *Works*, 1:713.

[41] Claude, *Essay*, 1:93.

[42] Claude, *Essay*, 1:4.

[43] Fuller did devote every Sunday to expounding larger portions of scripture, usually a chapter. His rules for these expositions differed from his rules for sermons, though the meaning of the text assumed priority in both cases. Fuller reflected on the benefit of these expositions to his Kettering congregation: "They have enabled us to take a more connected view of the Scriptures than could be obtained merely by sermons on particular passages; and I acknowledge that, as I have proceeded, the work of exposition has become more

After the text has been selected, Fuller advised his readers to "read it in connexion with the context, and endeavour by your own judgment to gain a clear idea of its genuine meaning."[44] Before the preacher may turn to outside help, he must deal with the text for himself. To do so, Fuller instructed, he should "examine the force of each word or term of importance."[45] For Claude, as for Fuller, difficult terms must be explained so as to ease any burdens caused by the text in the minds of the hearers.[46] Again, Fuller counseled his readers, "endeavor to understand a subject before you speak of it."[47] On this point, Fuller and Claude were in complete agreement, though his French counterpart offered a stricter warning: "No man will be so rash as to put pen to paper, or begin to discuss a text, till he has well comprehended the sense of it."[48] While understanding the meaning of the text does not guarantee a successful sermon, it does set the preacher on the path toward accuracy and clarity in his composition.

Provide the sermon with "a unity of design"

Once the meaning of the text is clear, the preacher must now shift his focus to designing his sermon. Claude outlined four potential options for the sermon's shape: explication, observation, application, or proposition.[49] In explicatory sermons, difficult subjects or terms are explained to remove any lingering confusion.[50] Texts or subjects that are easier to understand are discussed through a series of observations. Using this method, the preacher makes various theological observations that "instruct the mind" and "inflame the heart" of his listeners.[51] These first two options are labelled textuary sermons, "because, in effect, they keep to the text without digression, they regard it as the subject-matter of the whole discussion."[52]

In the applicational sermon, Claude counseled preachers to reduce the text

---

and more interesting to my heart." In Fuller, "Expository Discourses on the Book of Genesis," in *Works*, 3:1.

[44] Fuller, "Thoughts on Preaching: Letter III. The Composition of a Sermon," in *Works*, 1:718.

[45] Fuller, "Thoughts on Preaching: Letter III. The Composition of a Sermon," in *Works*, 1:718.

[46] Claude, *Essay*, 1:100.

[47] Fuller, "Thoughts on Preaching: Letter IV. The Composition of a Sermon" in Works, 1:724.

[48] Claude, *Essay*, 1:89.

[49] For a helpful discussion of Claude's four categories, see Rolf P. Lessenich, *Elements of Pulpit Oratory in Eighteenth-Century England (1660–1800)* (Köln, Germany: Böhlau-Verlag, 1972), 84–96.

[50] Claude, *Essay*, 1:99.

[51] Claude, *Essay*, 2:13.

[52] Claude, *Essay*, 2:325.

immediately to practice.[53] Verses that present simple commands that need no explanation fall into this category. The fourth and final option is the propositional sermon. In this method, the preacher focuses on subjects—formally stated as propositions—that arise from the text.[54] Whereas in the first two categories, the text was the field in which the preacher went to work, in the final two, the text is the home from which the preacher sets out on his journey.[55]

To what extent Fuller followed Claude's four categories is difficult to determine. Although he did not reproduce them exactly, he did carry several of Claude's principles with him into his own instructions. Fuller defined a sermon as "a discourse on some Divine subject, or a train of interesting thoughts on some sacred theme."[56] For him, sermons handled a variety of both doctrinal and practical subjects.[57] Although Fuller outlined three possible ways for a preacher to approach the sermon—topical, textual, or compound—only the topical and textual approaches are explained at length. In the preface to Fuller's letter on the topical method, the editor lamented that two other essays on the "Mixed and Applicatory mode of Composition" had been lost.[58] What Fuller might have said regarding these subjects remains unknown.

In both the textual and topical approaches, Fuller's primary concern was for the sermon to have a unity of design. He wrote that the preacher, "if he would interest a judicious hearer, must have an object at which he aims, and must never lose sight of it throughout his discourse."[59] For a topical sermon, the preacher asks, "What important truth is it that the text contains, and which I feel impressed upon my own mind, and wish to impress upon that of the congregation?"[60] To arrive at this truth, the preacher collects all his thoughts on the text and reduces them to a point.[61] This point, which Fuller recognized was formerly called the doctrine, comprises the primary subject of the discourse. Keith Grant, relying on Rolf Lessenich's work, connects Fuller's topical

---

[53] Claude, *Essay*, 2:325.

[54] Claude, *Essay*, 2:396.

[55] Claude, *Essay*, 2:325.

[56] Fuller, "Thoughts on Preaching: Letter IV. The Composition of a Sermon," in *Works*, 1:724.

[57] Fuller, "Thoughts on Preaching: Letter II. Sermons—Subject-Matter of Them," in *Works*, 1:714.

[58] Anonymous, "Preface" in *The Preacher; or Sketches of Original Sermons, Chiefly Selected from the Manuscripts of Two Eminent Divines of the Last Century, For the Use of Lay Preachers and Young Ministers*, ed. anonymous (Philadelphia, PA: J. Whetham, 1838), v.

[59] Fuller, "Thoughts on Preaching: Letter III. The Composition of a Sermon," in *Works*, 1:719.

[60] Fuller, "Thoughts on Preaching: Letter III. The Composition of a Sermon," in *Works*, 1:720.

[61] Fuller, "Thoughts on Preaching: Letter III. The Composition of a Sermon," in *Works*, 1:720.

approach to Claude's applicatory and propositional sermons.[62]

For texts that may not be reduced to a single topic, Fuller advised the preacher to "divide in a textual way, i.e. to propose to discourse first upon one part or branch of it; secondly, upon another."[63] Here again, Fuller's method loosely followed Claude's outlines for explicatory and observational sermons. At this point, it appears Grant is incorrect to equate Fuller's textual approach with his expositions and his topical approach with his sermons.[64] For Fuller, expositions and sermons formed two separate branches of the pastor's pulpit ministry. Properly speaking, the topical and textual approaches were both options for composing a sermon. It seems that Fuller employed a different approach to his expositions, which amounted to a running commentary on a larger portion of scripture.

Develop the "parts of the whole"

The final task of the preacher in composing his sermon is to develop its content. On this point, both Fuller and Claude stressed the importance of clarity and plain speech. "Embarrassment and obscurity," Claude warned, "are the most disagreeable thing in the world in a gospel-pulpit."[65] With sympathy for his audience, he continued, "It ought to be remembered, that the greatest part of the hearers are simple people, whose profit, however, must be aimed at in preaching: but it is impossible to edify them, unless you be very clear."[66] With matched enthusiasm, Fuller exhorted his readers, "A few well-chosen thoughts, matured, proved, and improved, are abundantly more acceptable than when the whole is chopped, as it were, into mince-meat."[67] If clarity is the objective, how does the preacher arrange his thoughts so that his sermon does not become a jumbled "mob of ideas?"[68]

To answer this question, Fuller referred his readers to the sermons of Jonathan Edwards, whose practice it was when preaching on a particular doctrine to illustrate, establish, and improve it. For his part, Edwards seems to have been

---

[62] Grant, *Andrew Fuller*, 84. See also Lessenich, *Elements of Pulpit Oratory*, 84.

[63] Fuller, "Thoughts on Preaching: Letter IV. The Composition of a Sermon" in Works, 1:724.

[64] Grant writes, "Following the general categories used by Claude and others, Fuller distinguished between expositions, characterized by "expounding the Scriptures," and sermons, described as 'discoursing on Divine subjects', the latter including both doctrinal and practical discourses. Or in other phrasing, he referred to them as "textual" and "topical" approaches to preaching" (Grant, *Andrew Fuller*, 84).

[65] Claude, *Essay*, 1:11.

[66] Claude, *Essay*, 1:11.

[67] Fuller, "Thoughts on Preaching: Letter IV. The Composition of a Sermon," in *Works*, 1:724.

[68] Fuller, "Thoughts on Preaching: Letter III: The Composition of a Sermon," in *Works*, 1:719.

influenced by the English Puritans who followed a similar method of doctrine, reason, and use.[69] In the first section of the sermon, the preacher illustrates, or explains, the subject he has derived from the text. He does this by offering several remarks in which the aim is to illuminate the truth for his people. Second, the preacher establishes his subject by offering various "evidences by which this important truth is supported."[70] Finally, he concludes by improving, or applying, the doctrine at hand. By crafting the sermon in this way, the preacher helps his people to answer three critical questions of the text: "What? Why? What then?"[71]

For his part, Claude outlined the sermon in three sections: the exordium (introduction), discussion, and application.[72] Explanations or observations on the text fill the majority of the discussion, depending on which approach the preacher has previously selected, while the application is reserved for practical instructions based on the truth that has been taught. For Claude, no sermon was complete until the truth had been applied. On this point, Lessenich observed, "The promotion of practical piety was the ultimate end of all neoclassical preaching, including the explicatory and the observatory sermons."[73] Doctrines give substance to practical piety and practical piety gives proof that the doctrines have taken root. Urging his own fellow ministers to preach in a similar way, Fuller wrote, "If you preach doctrinally, some may call you an Antinomian; if you preach practically, others may call you a legalist. But go on, my brother: this is a kind of dirt that won't stick. Preach the law evangelically, and the gospel practically."[74] Only when the twin realities of biblical truth and practical obedience have been clearly perceived by the people may the preacher rest assured that his task is complete.

Conclusion

The intent of this study has been to explore the influence of Jean Claude's *Essay*

---

[69] Grant cites the Puritan John Wilkins' work, *Ecclesiastes, or, A discourse concerning the gift of preaching as it falls under the rules of art* (Grant, *Andrew Fuller*, 86). See also "The Directory for Public Worship," in *The Westminster Confession* (1647, Edinburgh, UK: The Banner of Truth Trust, 2018); Horton Davies, *The Worship of the English Puritans* (Princeton, NJ: Soli Deo Gloria Publications, 1948).

[70] Fuller, "Thoughts on Preaching: Letter III. The Composition of a Sermon," in *Works*, 1:721.

[71] Fuller, "Thoughts on Preaching: Letter IV. The Composition of a Sermon," in *Works*, 1:725.

[72] Claude does mention two more parts, connection and division. Given that each of these are extremely short, he only "properly reckons" three. Curiously, he does not include the conclusion as one of his five parts to the sermon, even though he affords an entire chapter to it. In Claude, *Essay*, 1:1–2.

[73] Lessenich, *Elements of Pulpit Oratory*, 90.

[74] Fuller, "An Intimate and Practical Acquaintance with the Word of God," in *Works*, 1:485.

on the Composition of a Sermon on the homiletical method of Andrew Fuller. In his "Thoughts on Preaching," Fuller left behind a collection of letters in which he developed his theology of preaching and his process for preparing a sermon. Through these letters, Fuller shared Claude's vision that preachers are to instruct, please, and affect their hearers in every sermon. In addition to these three principal ends, Fuller prioritized Christ-centered preaching and the free offer of the Gospel in his instructions. Claude's deep concern for unity and clarity permeated Fuller's own instructions on preaching as he encouraged his readers to explain, establish, and improve the text for their people. As his homiletical guide, Claude supplied Fuller with a coherent method of sermon composition—one that he followed in his own preaching ministry and sought to impart to a younger generation.

Andrew Fuller's preaching on the Psalms

Nicholas J. Abraham

Nicholas J. Abraham is a PhD student at The Southern Baptist Theological Seminary, an Associate Pastor at Alpine Bible Church in Sugarcreek, Ohio, and an Instructor of Church History and Biblical Spirituality at Ohio Theological Institute. He can be reached at nabraham@ohiotheological.org.

"When I think of your rules from of old, I take comfort, O Lord" (Ps 119:52, ESV).[1] The psalmist's declaration of the enduring power and nature of the scriptures to give comfort to those that trust in YHWH is one which Christians should mark well. The Book of Psalms is, after all, in the Christian scriptures. As Sidney Greidanus has rightly stated, "The Old Testament and the New are both parts of the Christian Bible; both reveal the same covenant-making God; both reveal the gospel of God's grace; both show God reaching out to his disobedient children with the promise, 'I will be your God, and you will be my people'; both reveal God's acts of redemption."[2] In keeping with such an affirmation of the authority and relevance of the Old Testament--specifically the book of Psalms--the need is great for such scriptures to be preached in the Christian churches. Andrew Fuller (1754–1815) is a sound example of such kind of faithful preaching. This article explores Fuller's preaching on the Psalms by looking at his general approach, reviewing a sample of his psalm-sermons, and noting how his preaching of the Psalms can be emulated. It becomes evident that Fuller had a preference for preaching and teaching how to preach the Psalms. In his sermons, Fuller was faithful to the text while pointing to Jesus in the Psalms.

---

[1] All scriptural quotations in this article are from the King James Version, unless otherwise noted.

[2] Sidney Greidanus, *Preaching Christ from the Old Testament: A Contemporary Hermeneutical Method* (Grand Rapids, MI: Eerdmans, 1999), 45–46.

Fuller was comfortable preaching directly from the Psalms for the Christian life. Furthermore, Fuller preached the Psalms with appropriate pastoral sensitivity, and he followed the framework he taught concerning preaching, particularly in his Psalm-sermons.

Fuller's development in preaching
In late 1771 at the congregation that he would later pastor, Andrew Fuller stepped into the pulpit to fill in for the congregation's regular preacher at the time. The Particular Baptist chapel was located in the town of Soham in Cambridgeshire. Fuller's text for the morning was Psalm 30:5, "For his anger endureth but a moment; in his favour is life: weeping may endure for a night, but joy cometh in the morning." Fuller felt as if he was able to preach with "considerable freedom."[3] Soon after this occasion, Fuller preached at Soham for the second time, but it was over a year until he would preach there again.[4] The story of how he made it to the Soham pulpit as well as how he chose Psalm 30 from which to preach is of note.

The Soham congregation had recently been in the midst of turmoil. A church member was found to be grossly indulging in the drinking of alcohol. When questioned, the member's response smacked of antinomianism as he claimed that he lacked the ability to restrain himself from this sin. In the ensuing church disciplinary proceedings, the pastor, John Eve (d. 1782), made a comment stating his belief that Christians had the ability to do God's will. The Soham congregation embraced high-Calvinism and taught a view of God's sovereignty over man's responsibility—of which Fuller was thoroughly convinced at the time—so that they did not believe man's ability to do anything good apart from God.[5] Eve later resigned under the weight of pressure from a group in the

---

[3] Andrew Gunton Fuller, "Memoir," in *The Complete Works of the Rev. Andrew Fuller*, ed. Joseph Belcher (1845, repr., Harrisonburg, VA: Sprinkle, 1988), 1:11.

[4] Peter J. Morden, *The Life and Thought of Andrew Fuller (1754–1815)* (Milton Keynes, Buckinghamshire: Paternoster, 2015), 36.

[5] Fuller later shifted from this background of high Calvinism in relation to the issues that arose in the Soham church, namely the ability of man to do the will of God. Such a shift for preachers convinced of what John Eve espoused and later Fuller, would result in them calling people to do the will of God. Fuller began to move away from the high Calvinism of his youth due to his own thinking on this subject, in part due to the wisdom from other contemporary pastors he knew, and through reading Jonathan Edwards' (1703–1758), *Freedom of the Will* (1754) (Fuller, "Memoir," xxiii–xxv).

Regarding the sin of the church member, James Levit, and his response to Fuller's challenge posed to his sin, Peter Morden records, "Levit answered in a way that reveals the presence of antinomianism at Soham … To Fuller's consternation, Levit justified his behaviour by saying he could not help his drinking and did not have the power to keep himself from sin." According to the church, the pastor, John Eve, slipped up in his response, "In the course of the dispute, however, Eve made a comment to the effect that, whilst people had no power in and of themselves to anything spiritually good, they did have the power to obey the will of God

church. No replacement could be found and so the congregation decided to go forward without a regular pastor, and asked Joseph Diver (d. 1780) to act as a leading deacon.[6] Fuller recorded that Eve had resigned from the church in October 1771, which was not long before Fuller preached.[7]

On the day before he preached that first time at Soham, Fuller recorded that he was meditating on Psalm 30:5 as he traveled. He wrote, "I never had felt such freedom of mind in thinking on a Divine subject before; nor do I recollect ever having had a thought of the ministry; but then I felt as if I could preach from it, and indeed I did preach in a manner as I rode along."[8] It was the next morning, while on his way to church, Fuller discovered that he needed to preach. Fortunately, Fuller had his text and sermon prepared. Psalm 30:5 was an appropriate text, as it could speak to the difficulties the congregation had undergone. It is significant to notice that Fuller began his preaching career with the Psalms. Such a move displays Fuller's willingness to utilize the prayer-book of the Old Testament for Christian benefits. It is also significant to consider the content of the text Fuller selected, which displays a theme of God's comfort amidst affliction.

Fuller's sermons in the following few years at Soham seemed to have an impact, as he preached at the funeral of an elderly woman of the church by request in early 1774. For Peter Morden, this occasion marked a turning point that led the Soham congregation to call Fuller as their pastor.[9] By spring 1775, Fuller was called and ordained as the pastor of the Soham congregation.[10] Unfortunately, the extant sermons in Fuller's published works do not contain any preached from his time at Soham.[11] Of all of the sermons on the Psalms in Fuller's published works, the earliest dated sermon comes from just four years after his installation at Kettering in 1783.[12]

'as to outward acts'" (Morden, *Life and Thought of Andrew Fuller*, 36).

[6] Morden, *Life and Thought of Andrew Fuller*, 33–36.

[7] Fuller, *Works*, 1:10.

[8] Fuller, *Works*, 1:10–11.

[9] Morden, *Life and Thought of Andrew Fuller*, 36; Fuller, *Works*, 1:12.

[10] Fuller, *Works*, 1:14.

[11] Recently, progress has been made in deciphering Fuller's shorthand. This is significant because there were notebooks, which included sermons, that were previously unreadable. Such a development is also valuable because it makes accessible sermons from Fuller's time at Soham. At least two of these sermons have been published along with information about the deciphering of Fuller's shorthand in Stephen R. Holmes and Jonathan Woods, "Andrew Fuller's Soham Farewell Sermons: Context and Text," *Baptist Quarterly* 5.1 (2020): 2–16.

[12] Fuller, "Importance of Christian Ministers Considered as the Gift of Christ," *Works*, 1:521.

Thoughts on preaching: topical and textual
In a series of four undated letters, Andrew Fuller wrote to a young minister on the topic of preaching. These letters comprise a helpful look into Fuller's approach towards the pastoral task. The first letter is entitled, "Expounding the Scriptures," which expresses Fuller's general perspective of preaching.[13] The second letter is "Sermons–Subject Matter of Them," in which Fuller describes the necessity for the gospel to be preached in every sermon.[14] Both the third and fourth letters are entitled, "Composition of a Sermon," as they constitute a dual-part treatment of topical and textual sermons.[15]

In these letters, Fuller referred to preaching as a minister's "principal work," which he divided into two categories—"expounding the Scriptures and discoursing on Divine subjects."[16] The two categories serve for Fuller to be not only the tasks of a pastor in the pulpit, but also the two major sermon types to be regularly preached. Regarding the exposition of scripture, Fuller understood that the text should be preached in its context, thus in turn he wanted to convey that meaning to his audience. Fuller explained:

> If the hearer, when you have done, understand no more of that part of Scripture than he did before, your labour is lost. Yet this is commonly the case with those attempts at expounding which consist of little else than comparing parallel passages, or, by the help of a Concordance, tracing the use of the same word in other places, going from text to text till both the preacher and the people are wearied and lost. This is troubling the Scriptures rather than expounding them.[17]

Fuller wanted the scriptures to be understood first by the preacher, explained by the preacher, and then in turn understood by the listeners. He proposed that this understanding should come from "*drink*[ing] *in the spirit* of the writers."[18] It seems that Fuller sought after the authorial intent, yet he did not see it as a wooden, human action; instead, a Spirit-empowered one.[19] Furthermore, Fuller wanted to convey the need for preachers to read the scriptures "*as*

---

[13] Fuller, "Letter I, Expounding the Scriptures," *Works*, 1:712–714.

[14] Fuller, "Letter II, Sermons–Subject Matter of Them," *Works*, 1:714–717.

[15] Fuller, "Letter III, Composition of a Sermon," *Works*, 1:717–723; Fuller, "Letter IV, Composition of a Sermon," *Works*, 1:724–27.

[16] Fuller, *Works*, 1:712.

[17] Fuller, *Works*, 1:712.

[18] Fuller, *Works*, 1:713.

[19] Fuller stated, "It is by an *unction from the Holy One* that we know all things" (*Works*, 1:713).

a Christian."[20] In other words, Fuller encouraged his fellow preachers to have the texts soak into their souls.

In his second letter, Fuller discussed the subject matter of each sermon and the manner in which every sermon should be preached.[21] Fuller is careful to only refer to those addresses drawn from the exposition of scripture as sermons. Other addresses, though helpful and necessary at times, are not in Fuller's mind, sermons.[22] For Fuller, every sermon ought to focus on some aspect of the gospel and every sermon should be preached with the conviction and devotion such a gospel deserves.[23] Thus regarding sermons, Fuller stated:

> First, in every sermon we should have an errand; and one of such importance that if it be received or complied with it will issue in eternal salvation.
>
> Secondly, every sermon should contain a portion of the doctrine of salvation by the death of Christ.
>
> Thirdly, in preaching the gospel, we must not imitate the *orator*, whose attention is taken up with his performance, but rather the herald, whose object is to publish, or proclaim, good tidings.
>
> Fourthly, though the doctrine of reconciliation by the blood of Christ forms the ground-work of the gospel embassy, yet it belongs to the work of the ministry, not merely to declare that truth, but to accompany it with earnest calls, and pressing invitations, to sinners to receive it, together with the most solemn warnings and threatenings to unbelievers who shall continue to reject it.[24]

Considering all that Fuller had already stated, how does a sermon that fits the previously given criteria get composed? Interestingly, Fuller used a passage from the book of Psalms as his main example in both letters. For Fuller, there are three types of sermons: textual, topical, or compound.[25] He only gives explicit examples of the first two, but it seems that a compound sermon would be

---

[20] Fuller, *Works*, 1:714. Similarly, Joel Beeke also stated, "The Word of God is the heartbeat of our sanctification, the lifeline of our souls, and the foundation of our ministries" (*Reformed Preaching: Proclaiming God's Word from the Heart of the Preacher to the Heart of His People* (Wheaton, IL: Crossway, 2018), 372).

[21] Fuller, *Works*, 1:714.

[22] Fuller, *Works*, 1:714.

[23] Fuller, *Works*, 1:714–716.

[24] Fuller, *Works*, 1:715–717.

[25] Fuller, *Works*, 1:720.

some mixture of textual and topical. Each type begins with a careful exegesis of a passage, as for Fuller, exegesis of the scriptures is where preaching always begins. The first type of sermon that he described was the topical sermon. For his text, he used, "Thou openest thine hand, and satisfiest the desire of every living thing" (Ps 145:16). He began by seeking to understand the meaning of each word and what each word meant in relation to the others.[26] He contrasted the great themes he found in the verse with other biblical concepts.[27] He then sought to bring his thoughts together on the overall theme of the verse to drive towards the "leading sentiment" of the verse—in this example, he determined it to be "The bounty of Providence."[28] The overall structure is thus: "I. Explain the doctrine, II. Establish it, III. Improve it."[29] The first part of the structure is a basic overview of the doctrine—the doctrine of providence. The next part, establishing, which consists of providing evidence as to how the doctrine is so. In this case, it consists of observations made plainly in the world regarding the fact of God's providential working.[30] The final part of the structure explains what the doctrine of God's providence means for the lives of the hearers.[31]

In the final letter, Fuller described a textual sermon. He essentially followed the same structure as he did with the topical sermon, namely of explaining, establishing, and improving, but he made an important distinction—"in all cases the division must be governed by the materials you have to divide."[32] Fuller meant that certain texts or themes may require less explanation and possibly less evidence to support their validity, because they are so clear. At the foundation of what Fuller considered to be necessary to include are three questions he asked of any subject or text: "What? Why? What then?"[33] The questions are formed in a pattern themselves following much of how the apostle Paul presents truth in his epistles, namely that indicatives precede imperatives.[34] Additionally, Fuller made an important distinction about what to do with the "What?" portion of the sermon by arguing that an explanation of the text by itself is not

---

[26] Fuller, *Works*, 1:718.

[27] Fuller, *Works*, 1:718.

[28] Fuller, *Works*, 1:720.

[29] Fuller, *Works*, 1:721.

[30] Fuller, *Works*, 1:721–722.

[31] Fuller, *Works*, 1:722–723.

[32] Fuller, *Works*, 1:725.

[33] Fuller, *Works*, 1:725.

[34] Fuller refers to these two categories--indicative and imperative--as that which is "doctrinal" and that which is "practical" (see Fuller, *Works*, 1:725).

a sermon, but only a part.³⁵ In other words, Fuller believed that a sermon must explain what the text meant and then what is to be done by the hearers with what the text meant.³⁶ Fuller then used Psalm 36:9 as an example, as he saw this verse to be essentially saying, "the word of God is the grand medium by which we can attain a true and saving knowledge of God. What the sun and stars are to the regions of matter, that revelation is to the mental region."³⁷ The remainder of his example is quite similar to the topical sermon, except he continued to refer to aspects of the verse from which he started rather than only talking about the subject. In addition, Fuller only illustrated the aforementioned sum of the verse and then he sought to improve upon that illustration.³⁸

Importance of Christian Ministers considered as the gift of Christ (Ps 68:18)
When Fuller's sermons were published, only a few of their dates have been preserved. The following sermons are arranged chronologically when possible, and in a few instances, sermons of similar topics are grouped together.³⁹

The earliest sermon from the Psalms was preached at the occasion of William Carey's (1761–1834) ordination, which was from Psalm 68:18.⁴⁰ At the outset of the sermon, Fuller sought to show how this text was not merely meant for Israel, but Christians as well. Fuller sought to argue by referring to Paul's quotation and explanation of Psalm 68 in Ephesians 4.⁴¹ By distinguishing between the reception of gifts (Ps 68:18) and the giving of gifts (Eph 4:8), Fuller argued, "he received that he might give, received the spoil that he might distribute it."⁴² Fuller thus divided his sermon into two sections--first, he showed

---

³⁵ Fuller, *Works*, 1:724.

³⁶ One could say that Fuller followed a deductive model for preaching, by forming his sermons around an idea and presenting supporting points or information to support the main idea. His deductive development of sermons is in keeping with Haddon Robinson's descriptions of deductive sermons. See Haddon W. Robinson, *Biblical Preaching: The Development and Delivery of Expository Messages*, 3rd ed. (Grand Rapids, MI: Baker, 2014), 78–80.

³⁷ Fuller, *Works*, 1:724.

³⁸ Fuller, *Works*, 1:724–725.

³⁹ It is important to note that the sermons recorded in Fuller's *Works* are most likely abbreviated or shortened versions of the actual sermons preached. Also, the sermons left out of this essay are: "Public Worship" (Ps 68:26–28), "Prayer of David in the Decline of Life" (Ps 71:9), "Advantages of Early Piety" (Ps 90:14), "Past Trials a Plea for Future Mercies" (Ps 90:15), "The Vanity of the Human Mind" (Ps 94:11), and "Mysterious Nature of Man" (Ps 139:14).

⁴⁰ Fuller, "Importance of Christian Ministers Considered as the Gift of Christ," *Works*, 1:521–522. Belcher noted that the sermon was preached to the church in Moulton on August 1, 1787.

⁴¹ Fuller, *Works*, 1:521.

⁴² Fuller, *Works*, 1:521–522. Fuller went on to argue that ministers are received and given. They are

the gifts given by Christ to the church to be ministers; second, he charged the church to thankfully receive the gift of this minister.[43] In his defense of ministers being of the gifts given to the church, Fuller referred to the purpose clause of his main sermon text: "that the LORD God might dwell among them" (Ps 68:18). Fuller stated, "'Will God indeed dwell with men?' He will; and how? It is by the means of ordinances and ministers."[44] It is from this deep conviction of God's use of means, namely ministers, that Fuller ultimately charged the church to take hold of the means given them. As Michael Haykin and Brian Croft have pointed out, the regularity in Baptist churches at the time for ordination sermons was not only focused on the ordinand, but also on the church as to how they would receive their newly ordained pastor.[45] The church was charged to be faithful in attendance, to support their pastor, to seek peace, and to put away evil.[46]

A right spirit (Ps 51:10)
In this sermon, Fuller began with stating: "there was no period in David's life, in which he manifested more of the sinner, than in the case of Uriah; nor any in which he manifested more of the saint, than when he penned this psalm."[47] For Fuller, David's display of his position with the Lord came through his desire to be cleansed of sin, his desire to be holy, and he recognized that sin had clouded his mind regarding his position of grace.[48] This sermon was divided into three sections: first, that the text "contains a description of genuine religion;" second, that the text "teaches us that we are in danger of losing it;" and third, that the text "implies the necessity for its being renewed."[49] Genuine religion is displayed here through David's request for a "right spirit" (Ps 51:10). Fuller stated, "A right spirit is a spirit of love to God, and love to our neighbour, and

---

received in that Christ's death paid for such gifts and they are given by the Father as part of the blessings in Christ.

[43] Fuller, *Works*, 1:521–522.

[44] Fuller, *Works*, 1:522.

[45] Michael A.G. Haykin and Brian Croft, *Being a Pastor: A Conversation with Andrew Fuller* (Durham, England: Evangelical Press, 2019), 40.

[46] Fuller, *Works*, 1:522.

[47] Fuller, "A Right Spirit," *Works*, 3:836. Belcher noted that this sermon was preached at Ipswich on September 14, 1798.

[48] Fuller, *Works*, 3:836–837.

[49] Fuller, *Works*, 3:837.

a right disposition to ourselves."[50] David had none of these after his great sin, which was why he was drawn to repentance and was drawn to ask God for these things to be restored to his life. Next, Fuller described how David's request for this "right spirit" shows how he had obviously lost it. Fuller saw two types of danger in losing a right spirit, which are common and extraordinary. By common danger, Fuller meant the general danger that all with a sinful nature possess in being deadened to the things of God and then giving themselves to sin. By extraordinary danger, Fuller meant instances of intense temptation, like that of which David had undergone.[51] Finally, Fuller argued that this "right spirit" ought to be renewed through the gracious means God has provided in the Christian life and the church.[52] Outside of living in a right spirit, people can do nor receive any good, as people are vulnerable to great sin and have no real assurance of their salvation.[53] Fuller asked: "Is true religion an abiding work? Is it like a well of water springing up to everlasting life? Then it must flow somewhere. Its effects must be seen. Causes and effects must be united. Where true religion is begun, there will be suitable disposition and conduct."[54]

Nature and extent of true conversion (Ps 22:27)
Fuller summarized the prophetic nature of the Psalm, particularly its focus on the "sufferings of Christ and the glory that should follow" (1 Pet 1:11).[55] It is the glory that follows Christ's sufferings that Fuller claimed that the second part of the Psalm addressed. Thus, he argued, "the passage first read is a prediction of the conversion of the Gentiles."[56] From this conclusion, Fuller divided his sermon between the two themes of conversion's nature and extent.[57] For Fuller, conversion involves remembering, turning to the Lord, and worshipping. Remembering is about thinking about the sin that a person once walked in, which was once thought insignificant, of omission, or once thought of as good.[58] Conversion, on the other hand, is "turning to the Lord," which means one needs

---

[50] Fuller, *Works*, 3:837.

[51] Fuller, *Works*, 3:838–839.

[52] Fuller, *Works*, 3:839.

[53] Fuller, *Works*, 3:839–841.

[54] Fuller, *Works*, 3:841.

[55] Fuller, "Nature and Extent of True Conversion," *Works*, 1:549. Belcher noted that this sermon was preached in the circus at Edinburgh on October 13, 1799.

[56] Fuller, *Works*, 1:550.

[57] Fuller, *Works*, 1:550.

[58] Fuller, *Works*, 1:551.

to turn from sin to the Lord, which is necessary to salvation.[59] As for worship, Fuller explained: "if we be truly converted to Christ, we shall worship him both privately and publicly."[60]

With explaining the nature of conversion, Fuller turned to God's saving work being cast abroad through the church's obedience to the "Great Commission": "the coronation of Christ in heaven must be accompanied with the pardon of his murderers, and followed by the liberation of millions among the heathen who had hitherto been the willing captives of the prince of darkness."[61] Fuller concluded his sermon by appealing to his listeners to convert to Christ, and to the great missionary cause of taking the gospel to the nations, which he applied his eschatological perspectives on the widespread conversions to Christ in the days to come.[62]

Remedy for Mental Dejection (Ps 42:6)

Fuller began by considering the apostle John's exile on the island of Patmos.[63] The apostle was in a state of despair but was shown glorious things about what was to come, so to encourage him. By linking David and the apostle, Fuller stated: "David is now in that state which John beheld, clothed in white robes, and with palms of victory in his hands; but David a little while ago was passing this life in great tribulation."[64] Fuller thus divided his sermon into under two headings: first, there will be times when people will have their souls cast down; and second, a noted remedy from scripture for the downcast soul is to look back on God in the past as to how he brought deliverance before.[65]

As for the first heading, Fuller examined the various causations of people's experience of downcast souls. For Fuller, such an experience may be caused: when "the hand of the Lord goeth out against us;"[66] when God refuses communion with his people for a time;[67] when one's conscience is burdened with

---

[59] Fuller, *Works*, 1:551–552.

[60] Fuller, *Works*, 1:552.

[61] Fuller, *Works*, 1:552.

[62] Fuller, *Works*, 1:552–553.

[63] Fuller, "Remedy for Mental Dejection," *Works*, 1:368–374. Belcher noted that this sermon was preached at Carter-lane meeting house in London on March 24, 1800.

[64] Fuller, *Works*, 1:368.

[65] Fuller, *Works*, 1:369.

[66] Fuller, *Works*, 1:369.

[67] Fuller, *Works*, 1:370.

guilt;[68] or when God does not bless the labors of his people.[69] Fuller reminded that there are even more painful cases where all of these cases coincide together in the life of a believer at the same time.[70] Understanding the causations, Fuller then turned to the remedy. With the Psalmist, Fuller understood that the source of comfort is God, as "God must be the object in which our faith and hope and joy must centre."[71] By examining how the patriarchs turned to God amid sorrows, Fuller then sought to directly address his hearers:

> The church at Ephesus was exhorted to remember how she had heard, and how she had received the word of God. O dejected Christian! do thou also remember how thou hast heard; call to recollection thy former sorrows, thy former hopes, thy former joys, thy former confidences, not in order to seek comfort without a renewal of them, but with a view to rekindle, if it be possible, the lost flame; to recall the former joys, the former hopes, the former confidences, that the things may be revived which are ready to die; this will do thy soul good under all thy dejections.[72]

In addition, Fuller pointed out the location that David could not have looked—Calvary, about which Fuller stated: "Remember him from Gethsemane and Calvary; and if that be not a relief, nothing can be."[73] Thus, Fuller called his Christian hearers to look to Christ amid their burdens and sorrows.

Solitary reflection (Ps 4:4)
Fuller's intent in this sermon was to call the congregation to properly deal with the Lord, as he pointed out: "Religion is not found among noise, and clamour, and dispute. It does not consist in either applauding or censuring men. If ever you hear to any purpose, it will make you forget the preacher, and think only of yourselves. You will be like a smitten deer, which, unable to keep pace with the herd, retires to the thicket and bleeds alone."[74]

Fuller then explained the meaning of the text and enforced its meaning

---

[68] Fuller, *Works*, 1:371.

[69] Fuller, *Works*, 1:371.

[70] Fuller, *Works*, 1:372.

[71] Fuller, *Works*, 1:372.

[72] Fuller, *Works*, 1:372–374.

[73] Fuller, *Works*, 1:374.

[74] Fuller, "Solitary Reflection," *Works*, 1:221–228. Belcher did not record a date for this sermon, but he did note that it was preached on a Lord's-day evening in a country village. Based on the context of the sermon, it seems as though Fuller may have been a visiting preacher on this occasion.

upon the congregation.[75] Fuller defined the original recipients of Psalm 4 as enemies of David; thus, contemporary recipients are those who are enemies of Jesus.[76] To help his audience, Fuller posed several questions, with which, Fuller aimed to help his audience to understand and reflect the relationship between their heart and conscience, the source of their conscience, their pursuits and satisfaction, and their eternal state.[77] To aid his unbelieving audience, Fuller exhorted them to think and mediate on what he preached carefully. With four applications, Fuller concluded by saying, "if you commune with your heart to any good purpose, you will never think of being saved by the works of your own hands; but feel the necessity of a Saviour, and of a great one. The doctrine of salvation by the death of Jesus will be glad tidings to your soul."[78] For Fuller, such a call to look to Christ is the same call Psalm 4:5.[79]

Advice to the Dejected (Ps 13:2)
Fuller argued that help for sorrow may not always come from focusing within one's heart.[80] Fuller divided his sermon into two sections: considering the state of the psalmist's condition and what he did to deal with it, and how the same solution could be applied to his hearers.[81]

Regarding the first section, Fuller examined the psalm's context.[82] He saw that Psalm 13 was about the great trial that David faced under Saul.[83] Fuller argued that in amidst his trial, David found help "by ceasing to take counsel

---

[75] Fuller, *Works*, 1:221.

[76] Fuller, *Works*, 1:221.

[77] Fuller, *Works*, 1:222–225.

[78] Fuller, *Works*, 1:228.

[79] Fuller, *Works*, 1:228.

[80] Fuller, "Advice to the Dejected," *Works*, 1:228–236. Belcher did not add any editorial note to this sermon for place or time.

[81] Fuller, *Works*, 1:228.

[82] For the context of Psalm 13, it seems that Fuller was informed by the superscription, which notes it as a Psalm of David. Allan Moseley has argued, referring to Tremper Longman's work, against allowing the superscriptions to drive one's exposition of a Psalm. See Allan Moseley, *From the Study to the Pulpit: An 8-Step Method for Preaching and Teaching the Old Testament* (Bellingham, WA: Lexham, 2017), 114–115. Richard Gamble has engaged with this concern for using superscriptions and noted that there has been recent work done to show the superscriptions are actually quite earlier than some have thought. Gamble considers the superscriptions as valid for studying the Psalms. See Richard C. Gamble, *The Whole Counsel of God*, Vol. 1, *God's Mighty Acts in the Old Testament* (Phillipsburg, NJ: P&R, 2009), 1:520.

[83] Fuller, *Works*, 1:228–230.

in his soul, and by looking out of himself, and trusting in the mercy of God."[84] Fuller then moved to the second section of his sermon wherein he sought to determine how David's relief is something for which Christians can hope to find in the same way. He summarized three different types of people that may find relief from the Lord as David did: those suffering under unfavorable conditions of God's providence; those caught up in darkness and a kind of spiritual depression; and those that struggle to find assurance of their salvation.[85] For each of these types of persons, Fuller concluded that God can deliver them as he delivered David:

> Read the Holy Scriptures, pray to the Fountain of light for understanding, attend the preaching of the word; and all this is not with the immediate view of determining what you are, but what Christ is; and if you find in him that in which you whole soul acquiesces, this, without your searching after it, will determine the question as to your personal interest in him.[86]

While this charge was intently relevant to the person struggling with assurance, it is certainly relevant to every kind of person Fuller mentioned, because the charge was for such a person to look to Christ.

The conduct of David in trouble (Ps 40:1–3)
Fuller stated that without the Psalms Christians would be left feeling alone in their various emotions directed towards God, but the Psalms provide the church with hope in these emotions.[87] Fuller summarized his thoughts into four categories: first, "The situation of the Psalmist;" second, "His conduct under it;" third, "The answer, or his deliverance from it;" and fourth, how Fuller's hearers can apply this to their own lives.[88] Fuller understood the psalmist's situation as being delivered from focusing on sin instead of on God's mercy.[89] The psalmist's response in the pit—to pray, to cry out to God—was understood

---

[84] Fuller, *Works*, 1:230.

[85] Fuller, *Works*, 1:230–234.

[86] Fuller, *Works*, 1:236.

[87] Fuller, "The Conduct of David in Trouble," *Works*, 1:379–384. Belcher noted that this was preached at Eagle Street in London on a Wednesday evening, dated June 18, 1800. He also noted that the sermon in the *Works* was from notes taken by W.B. Gurney.

[88] Fuller, *Works*, 1:379.

[89] Fuller, *Works*, 1:380.

as the normal response of God's people.⁹⁰ In response, God delivered psalmist by hearing his cry.⁹¹ Fuller thus appealed to the congregation: "Do you sink in deep mire? Are you plunged, from whatever cause, as into a horrible pit? You are thereby taught by the example of the Psalmist to put your trust in God; from his example take comfort, and charm your griefs to rest."⁹² In this final charge, Fuller called the listeners to have faith in Christ amid their grief.

Desire for the success of God's cause (Ps 90:16–17)
According to Belcher, this sermon was preached at the opening of a new Baptist meeting house at Boston in Lincolnshire on June 25, 1801. Fuller began by relating the present situation of his preaching for the new meeting house to the Psalm's concern about God's work.⁹³ The first part of Fuller's sermon dealt with the things desired by Moses and the second part of the sermon dealt with how desirable these things are.⁹⁴ For Moses, the first thing he desired was God's work would be visible, about which Fuller stated that it could be visible through sinners' conversion and Christians' growth in grace.⁹⁵ The second thing Moses desired was God's glory to be seen through his work.⁹⁶ The third thing was that God would be showed as beautiful.⁹⁷ The fourth thing was for God to establish his servants' work.⁹⁸ The fifth thing was for these things to be fulfilled in their own time.⁹⁹

Regarding how desirable these things were, Fuller stated that God's glory would be shown with the work of gospel ministry bringing about the kingdom of God.¹⁰⁰ In light of this point, Fuller pointed out that the progresses and development in mission are connected to the health and progress of the church.¹⁰¹

---

[90] Fuller, *Works*, 1:381.

[91] Fuller, *Works*, 1:382.

[92] Fuller, *Works*, 1:384.

[93] Fuller, *Works*, 1:413–417.

[94] Fuller, *Works*, 1:414.

[95] Fuller, *Works*, 1:414–415.

[96] Fuller, *Works*, 1:415.

[97] Fuller, *Works*, 1:415.

[98] Fuller, *Works*, 1:416.

[99] Fuller, *Works*, 1:416.

[100] Fuller, *Works*, 1:416.

[101] Fuller, *Works*, 1:416.

Finally, Fuller stated that these desired things ought to be commended and practiced through the ministry of the church.[102]

Jesus the true Messiah (Ps 40:6–8)
In this sermon, Fuller began by stating the division between Jews and Christians regarding the Messiah was "not whether the Scriptures predict and characterize the Messiah, but whether these predictions and characters be fulfilled in Jesus."[103] For Fuller, there are three characteristics in Psalm 40 to mark the Messiah's coming, which are "that the sacrifices and ceremonies of the Mosaic law would thence be superseded; that the great body of Scripture prophecy would be accomplished; and that the will of God would be perfectly fulfilled."[104]

For Fuller, though Jews claim the continuance of the ceremonial law, such a belief is contrary to the scriptures. To prove his point, Fuller quoted a litany of biblical passages.[105] Furthermore, Fuller noted how the author of Hebrews quoted Jeremiah 31:31–34 and referred to the Mosaic covenant as old (Heb 8:13).[106] Fuller also argued that the ceremonial sacrifices had been stopped at the destruction of Jerusalem and the temple.[107]

Second, Fuller argued that the multitude of prophecies in the Old Testament have been accomplished in Jesus.[108] These prophecies were about the time and place of the Messiah's coming, the family to which the Messiah belonged, the kind of miracles he should perform, his lowliness as a king, his suffering and death, his resurrection, and his rejection by his own people and his kingdom being among the Gentiles.[109] Finally, Fuller argued that Jesus did the will of

---

[102] Fuller, *Works*, 1:417.

[103] Fuller, "Jesus the True Messiah," *Works*, 1:210–220. Belcher noted that this sermon was preached in the Jews' Chapel, which belonged to a group called The London Society for Promoting the Conversion of the Jews, on Church Street in Spitalfields on November 19, 1809.

[104] Fuller, *Works*, 1:210.

[105] Fuller, *Works*, 1:211. The passages he quoted were 1 Sam 15:22, Ps 50:11–15, Ps 51:16–17, Isa 1:11–12, Jer 7:21–23, and Dan 9:27.

[106] Fuller, *Works*, 1:211–212.

[107] Fuller, *Works*, 1:212.

[108] Walter Kaiser has made similar arguments as to the prophets giving clear accounts about the Messiah. Kaiser provided a similar list of things as Fuller did in his sermon that were clear to prophets about the Messiah. The clarity that the prophets had about various aspects of the Messiah only gives more proof to Jesus indeed being the Messiah. See Walter C. Kaiser Jr., *Preaching and Teaching from the Old Testament: A Guide for the Church* (Grand Rapids, MI: Baker, 2003), 41.

[109] Fuller, *Works*, 1:213–216.

God, which was by conforming his life to divine precepts.[110] Fuller dealt with certain Jewish claims about Jesus: that Jesus was not the Messiah, that he had not fulfilled various messianic prophecies, that he was not for peace, that he pretended to be the Son of God, and that some of Jesus' teachings were not practical or possible.[111] Fuller argued that Jewish contentions against Jesus as Messiah did not take into consideration the timing described in passages like Isaiah 9:7: "But it is not said that these effects should immediately follow his appearing. On the contrary, there was to be an increase of his government; yea, a continued increase."[112] As for accusations that Jesus was not for peace, Fuller showed from the examples of Abel, Hezekiah, and Moses that any lack of peace surrounding Jesus came from those who rejected him.[113] Regarding Jesus pretending to be the Son of God, Fuller showed from Psalm 2 that for Jesus to be the Messiah was synonymous with being the Son of God.[114] Fuller also said that any accusation that Jesus's teachings were not practical came from a focus on the letter of the law of Christ rather than its spirit.[115] In conclusion, Fuller called his hearers to believe on Jesus and called Christians to pursue the heart of Christ for the lost.[116]

Assessment

To conclude this study of Fuller's preaching on the Psalms, some observations are worth noting. First, it can be observed that Fuller had a preference for the book of Psalms. As it was mentioned, Fuller preached his first sermon from the Psalter, and later he used it to convey the basics of preaching for young ministers. Among Fuller's published sermons, fifteen of the ninety-four were from the Psalter. Statistically, it reveals a particular emphasis on this book. Furthermore, Fuller mentioned in his diary a long stint of time when he had been preaching through the Psalms and found pleasure in doing so.[117] Additionally, among the sermons located in Fuller's notebook that were previously unreadable, there are more sermons from the Psalms than from any other book in the

---

[110] Fuller, *Works*, 1:217.

[111] Fuller, *Works*, 1:218–219

[112] Fuller, *Works*, 1:218.

[113] Fuller, *Works*, 1:218–219.

[114] Fuller, *Works*, 1:219.

[115] Fuller, *Works*, 1:219.

[116] Fuller, *Works*, 1:220.

[117] Fuller stated, "From last April I have been expounding the book of Psalms, and sometimes have enjoyed pleasure therein" (Fuller, "Memoir," liii)

Bible.[118] Fuller's preference for the Psalms helps highlight its value for Christian preaching.

Second, Fuller preached from the Psalms by displaying a proper sensitivity to the tenor of the text. For Fuller, he sought to first understand the context, which then directed the contour of his exposition. Each of the sermons listed above began with explaining the psalm's context, which was maintained throughout the sermon. Such a practice was commended by Fuller, as he encouraged preachers to "drink in the spirit of the writers."[119] As a result, Fuller avoided using a single verse as a springboard to preach his preferred topic. With a focal point of a text, Fuller preached "where the passage's theme or point of view comes out in its fullest expression."[120]

Third, Fuller preached the Psalms with an effective pastoral sensitivity to his audience no matter the occasion—either at William Carey's ordination, to the society concerned with reaching Jews for Christ, in his two sermons delivered as a visiting pastor, or at the dedication of a new church building. From his sermons, it can be observed that Fuller loved "God's people and [knew] their spiritual state, their needs, their hungers, their yearnings."[121]

Fourth, Fuller consistently preached the biblical texts as the way he summarized in his letters to a young minister. Fuller regularly preached from the Psalms with an errand present in his sermon, with a focus on the death of Christ, with the task of a herald, and with great pleas for his hearers to trust in the Lord.[122] For example, from Psalm 40 and David's example Fuller called on his hearers to trust in the Lord amid their grief.[123] His basic pattern of "What? Why? What then?" can also be found in his sermons in terms of how he structured his messages.[124] This pattern was displayed in his message on Psalm 90 as Fuller showed in Moses's petitions the objects he desired through prayer and that such objects were desirable for his hearers as well. As Fuller stated, "Every subject, in some degree, requires a mode of discussion for itself," gave way for the flexibility, as testified in the above examples.[125] Such flexibility came

---

[118] Michael A.G. Haykin, email to author, August 13, 2020.

[119] Fuller, *Works*, 1:713.

[120] Kaiser, *Preaching and Teaching from the Old Testament*, 55, 157.

[121] Abraham Kuruvilla, *A Manual for Preaching: The Journey from Text to Sermon* (Grand Rapids, MI: Baker, 2019), 64.

[122] Fuller, *Works*, 1:715–717.

[123] Fuller, *Works*, 1:384.

[124] Fuller, *Works*, 1:725.

[125] Fuller, *Works*, 1:725.

through in his message on Psalm 13 wherein Fuller needed to derive context from the rest of the Psalm, but also from the context of his hearers as to why they come upon such periods of despondency.[126]

Fifth, Fuller preached on the Christian life directly from the Psalms. In his sermon for Carey's ordination, Fuller used Psalm 68:18 to articulate how a church should treat and esteem its pastor. From Psalm 51, Fuller gave a description of "genuine religion."[127] Fuller made a clear appeal to true conversion from Psalm 22. In sum, he was able to commend the life shaped by the gospel from the Psalter.

Finally, Fuller preached Jesus from the Psalms. In each of the examples, Fuller brought the congregation to consider Christ in some way with the text from which he preached. This was most explicit in the final sermon mentioned, "Jesus The True Messiah." However, he also closed with a call to trust in Christ in his sermon on Psalm 4: "If you commune with your heart to any good purpose, you will never think of being saved by the works of your own hands; but feel the necessity of a Saviour, and of a great one."[128] Such calls were commonplace among his preaching on the Psalms and his preaching at large. Fuller's conviction to preach Christ was rooted in another source, which was his statement of faith submitted to the church in Kettering upon his installation as pastor. Fuller declared in this statement, "I believe it is the duty of every minister of Christ plainly and faithfully to preach the gospel to all who will hear it."[129] Significantly, Fuller did not see a situation in which a Christian preacher would not preach Jesus. A conviction to preach the gospel by calling all to repent and believe in Christ transformed his preaching style while at Soham. This change came as a result of his shift away from high Calvinism towards a burden to give the free offer of the gospel to all as is articulated in *The Gospel Worthy of All Acceptation*.[130] Not only did Fuller have conviction about the need to preach the gospel to all, but he had a conviction that Jesus and the gospel could be preached from all of scripture.[131] Fuller believed that like the rest of scriptures,

---

[126] Fuller, *Works*, 1:228–230.

[127] Fuller, *Works*, 3:837.

[128] Fuller, *Works*, 1:228.

[129] Michael A.G. Haykin, ed., *The Armies of the Lamb: The spirituality of Andrew Fuller* (Dundas, ON: Joshua, 2001), 279.

[130] Robert W. Oliver, *History of the English Calvinistic Baptists 1771–1892* (Edinburgh: Banner of Truth, 2006), 94. See also Fuller, *Works*, 2:383–393.

[131] Fuller established this in his "Thoughts on Preaching" by showing the need for any scriptural preaching to be gospel preaching. Furthermore, any gospel preaching must be either the preaching of the gospel or preaching some truth supposed by the gospel or some other doctrines related to it. This kind of preaching could be done from any place in the Scriptures. See Fuller, *Works*, 1:716.

the Psalter is about Jesus. Thus, Christian preachers need to preach Christ from the Psalter (Luke 24:27).

Thomas Scott and the Baptists

Timothy Warren Scott

Timothy Scott is the pastor of Salem Baptist Church in Florissant, MO and an adjunct professor of philosophy at Missouri Baptist University.

This past April marked the bicentennial anniversary of the death of an Anglican minister named Thomas Scott (1747–1821).[1] At the time of his passing, Scott was one of the most recognizable names in evangelical Christianity. This was a man who had, at least for a while, pastored the likes of William Wilberforce (1759–1833). He had also been the first secretary of the Church Missionary Society (CMS), and his books had sold thousands of copies in both England and the United States. In particular, his personal conversion story, *The Force of Truth* (1779),[2] became something of an evangelical classic, and

---

[1] For biographical information on Thomas Scott, see Andrew Crichton, *Memoirs of the Rev. Thomas Scott, Late Rector of Aston Sandford Bucks: With General Remarks on His Life, Character, and Writings* (Edinburgh: H.S. Baynes, 1825); A.C. Downer, *Thomas Scott the Commentator* (London: Charles J. Thynne, 1909); Charles Hole, "A Memoir of the Rev. Thomas Scott," unpublished manuscript CMS/ACC87 D17 [Cadbury Research Library at the University of Birmingham, Birmingham, UK]; Marcus L. Loane, *Oxford and the Evangelical Succession* (London: Lutterworth Press, 1950), 132–191; John Scott, *The Life of the Rev. Thomas Scott, D.D., Rector of Aston Sandford, Bucks: Including a Narrative Drawn Up by Himself and Copious Extracts of His Letters*, 6th ed. (London: L.B. Seeley, 1824); Mary Seeley, *The Later Evangelical Fathers: John Thornton, John Newton, William Cowper, Thomas Scott, Richard Cecil, William Wilberforce, Charles Simeon, Henry Martyn, Josiah Pratt* (London: Seeley, Jackson, & Halliday, 1879), 150–187. There is also some helpful biographical information in the two funeral sermons Daniel Wilson preached for Thomas Scott. See Daniel Wilson, *Sermons and Tracts* (London: George Wilson, 1825), 1:475–591.

[2] Thomas Scott, *The Force of Truth: An Authentic Narrative* (London: G. Keith, 1779); Thomas Scott,

Scott's *Family Bible*,[3] a commentary on the entirety of Scripture, could be found in many evangelical households. Even John Henry Newman (1801–1890), of Oxford Movement fame, wept at one of Scott's funeral services; and though Newman later left the Church of England for Roman Catholicism, he still wrote affectionately of Scott, saying he was "the writer who made a deeper impression on my mind than any other, and to whom (humanly speaking) I almost owe my soul."[4]

Sadly, the evangelical memory of Thomas Scott has faded over the years. Today, few people outside of specialized historians have probably ever heard his name, and his contributions to evangelical history have been overshadowed by some of his more famous contemporaries. This "Thomas Scott amnesia" is certainly regrettable for evangelicals who are members of the Church of England, as Scott left them a strong legacy of biblical fidelity and missionary zeal. However, it could be argued that Baptists too should take more notice of Scott's life, as his interactions with Baptists made a small, but important contribution to their history. Like his friend John Newton (1725–1807), who was well-known for making friends in other denominations,[5] Scott possessed a catholic[6] spirit that brought him into cordial relationships with several prominent Baptist figures and enabled the respective parties to enjoy mutual help and encouragement. In this essay, Scott's Baptist friendships, together with his involvement in the Baptist Missionary Society (BMS), will be reviewed. The goal of this review

---

The Holy Bible, Containing the Old and New Testaments: With Original Notes, and Practical Observations (London: Bellamy and Robarts, 1788–1792). *The Force of Truth* is significant in the history of evangelicalism because it fostered the development of a literary genre known as the "evangelical conversion narrative." For a detailed study of this genre, see D. Bruce Hindmarsh, *The Evangelical Conversion Narrative: Spiritual Autobiography in Early Modern England* (Oxford: Oxford University Press, 2005).

[3] Thomas Scott, *The Holy Bible, Containing the Old and New Testaments: With Original Notes, and Practical Observations* (London: Bellamy and Robarts, 1788–1792). According to G.R. Balleine, Scott's *Commentary* sold over 37,000 copies in Scott's lifetime (*A History of the Evangelical Party in the Church of England* (London: Longmans, Green, and Co., 1911), 81).

[4] John Henry Cardinal Newman, *Apologia Pro Vita Sua and Six Sermons*, ed. Frank M. Turner (New Haven, CT: Yale University Press, 2008), 134.

[5] See Geoffrey F. Nuttall, "Baptists and Independents in Olney to the Time of John Newton," *Baptist Quarterly* 30 (1983): 26–37. Newton was known especially for his extensive correspondence with Christians from many different religious backgrounds. In terms of Baptist history, one notable example was the mentoring relationship Newton had with John Ryland, Jr. The two ministers maintained a lengthy correspondence in which they discussed a multitude of issues related to pastoral ministry. See Grant Gordon, ed., *Wise Counsel: John Newton's Letters to John Ryland, Jr.* (Edinburgh: The Banner of Truth Trust, 2009).

[6] The term *catholic* is used here in reference to the belief that all true Christians are members of the universal or catholic Church, no matter their denominational affiliation. Thus, a catholic spirit includes a friendliness and love for all members of the cniversal Church. The term is not intended as a reference to the Roman Catholic Church.

is to show that a strong catholic spirit existed between Scott and his Baptist counterparts in the long eighteenth century.[7]

During the course of his life, Thomas Scott pastored in several English parishes, including Olney, London, and Aston Sandford. Each of these ministry stations brough him into contact with Baptist ministers and laypersons who helped him develop a network of Baptist friendships throughout the country. Some of these friendships were of a more of casual nature, such as those he had with men such as Andrew Fuller (1754–1815) and William Carey (1764–1834). However, Scott's friendship with John Ryland, Jr. (1753–1825) was much deeper, and the two men could easily have been described as "best friends," even though they ministered in different denominations. In this section, Scott's Baptist friendships will be surveyed in order to show how Scott's catholic spirit was manifested at the personal level.

Andrew Fuller

The first friendship to be examined is the one Scott made with Andrew Fuller. It is likely that Scott had met Fuller sometime prior to 1786, since Scott mentioned having a deep affection for him in a letter to John Ryland Jr., dated May 24, 1786. In the letter, Scott wrote, "I trust I can truly say that I also have the welfare of all the friends of truth and holiness near my heart; and I know but few in my own line, that I feel more cordially united to, than yourself, Mr. Fuller, and Mr. Symmonds."[8] Regrettably, few details of how they came to know one another or how often they interacted remain. However, it is known that Scott hosted Fuller in his London home in 1792. In this instance, Fuller told Scott about "the impression which had been made upon an association meeting of his own denomination, by Mr. Carey's sermon on the address to the church, (Isaiah liv.2,), *Lengthen thy cords, and strengthen thy stakes;* from which he pressed the two propositions, that we should *expect* great things, and *attempt* great things."[9] Fuller was, of course, describing the sermon Carey preached on May 31, 1792, at the Northampton Baptist Association's annual meeting, which played an important part in the formation of the BMS later that year. As such, Scott received a first-hand account of one of the most important meetings in Baptist history from Fuller; and it seems nearly certain that the subject of

---

[7] The phrase "long eighteenth century" is historical shorthand for the period in British history dating from the Glorious Revolution of 1688 to the Reform Act of 1832. However, the exact dates referenced might vary slightly among historians. This phraseology is preferrable in this context to the narrower "eighteenth century" because Scott lived until 1821.

[8] Thomas Scott, Letter to John Ryland, Jr., May 24, 1786, The Scott Family Correspondence to John Ryland, 1786–1825 (Bristol Baptist College, Bristol, UK).

[9] Scott, *Life of Thomas Scott*, 174.

foreign missions was among the topics of conversation. This friendly interaction between Fuller and Scott is notable because it took place between the men who would later become the first secretaries of the BMS and the CMS respectively.

William Carey

Not only was Scott a friend of the BMS's first secretary; he also befriended the BMS's first missionary, William Carey. Like in the case with Fuller, the details of Scott's relationship with Carey are rather scant, but it is worth noting that Scott played an important role early on in Carey's conversion. Carey was around fifteen years old when he first met Scott; and at the time, Carey was beginning to come to grips with his own sinful condition. As Carey was wrestling though this issue, he was influenced by Scott's preaching. According to the *Bengal Obituary*, the young Carey had "occasional access to the ministration of the Rev. Thomas Scott," and Scott's preaching "tended greatly to increase his convictions of his fallen condition."[10] Carey himself later described the role Scott played in his conversion in a letter to John Ryland, Jr., in which he wrote, "If there be anything of the work of God in my soul, I owe much of it to [Scott's] preaching when I first set out in the ways of the Lord."[11]

The relationship between the two men later deepened when Carey was apprenticed to Thomas Old of Hackleton, who was Scott's good friend.[12] Scott customarily made visits to Old's residence several times a year; and consequently, he would have been able to get to know Carey more intimately. There is little doubt that Scott greatly admired Carey, and he later wrote that he had "from the first thought young Carey an extraordinary person."[13] For the remainder of his life, Scott closely followed the news about Carey's missionary endeavors, and Scott borrowed much in terms of missionary methodology from Carey's work in India.

The Haddenham Baptists

A lesser-known example of Scott's Baptist friendships is his relationship with

---

[10] *The Bengal Obituary; or, A Record to Perpetuate the Memory of Departed Worth: Being a Compilation of Tablets and Monumental Inscriptions from Various of the Bengal and Agra Presidencies, to Which is Added Biographical Sketches and Memoirs of Such as Have Pre-Eminently Distinguished Themselves in the History of British India Since the Formation of the European Settlement to the Present Time* (London: W. Thacker & Co., 1851), 334.

[11] Scott, *Life of Thomas Scott*, 173.

[12] See Mary Drewery, *William Carey* (Grand Rapids: Zondervan, 1978), 20.

[13] Thomas Scott, Letter to Joseph Ivimey, January 31, 1815, quoted in Drewery, *William Carey*, 20.

the Baptists who worshipped at the Baptist Meeting House in Haddenham.[14] For the last twenty years of his life, Scott ministered in a small village north of London known as Aston Sandford. Nearby was the village of Haddenham; and around the year 1809, Andrew Fuller and several other Baptists attempted to revive a Baptist church that had mostly fizzled out there. Scott had reason to take notice of this effort, as one of the key leaders among the Baptists frequently attended Scott's church at Aston Sandford. In a letter to John Ryland, Jr., Scott reported that "the person, who has the meeting rebuilt … and will probably in due time be pastor, has been and is one of my most constant hearers, and most attached disciples, saving that he is a Dissenter and a Baptist *sui generis*."[15] Scott apparently thought highly of his Baptist disciple, and he described him as "a truly pious young man."[16]

Yet, Scott also recognized that the formation of a new church in the sparsely populated area of Aston Sandford and Haddenham could spell trouble for his own church. "I foresee," he told Ryland, "that, when God shall remove me; unless someone succeeds me, of considerable influence, the church at Aston will be deserted for the Meeting at Haddenham."[17] What is remarkable is Scott's attitude in response to this possibility. Instead of being upset by the prospect, he very graciously stated, "What shall I say? Why, if God puts the poor sinners in this neighbourhood, by my ministry, among his children, (as I trust he does a considerable number); he has full right to train up his own children, in his own way, for their heavenly inheritance."[18] In this situation, Scott's catholic spirit was once again on display, and the Baptist Meeting House in Haddenham was blessed to have its eventual pastor mentored by Scott.

John Ryland, Jr.
The clearest and best-known example of Scott's friendship with Baptist leaders

---

[14] Much of what follows in this section has been adapted from my dissertation. See Timothy Warren Scott, "Thomas Scott and Evangelical Missions" (PhD dissertation, The Southern Baptist Theological Seminary, 2018), 172–73.

[15] Thomas Scott, Letter to John Ryland, Jr., December 18, 1809, The Scott Family Correspondence to John Ryland, 1786–1825.

[16] Thomas Scott, Letter to John Ryland, Jr., December 18, 1809.

[17] Thomas Scott, Letter to John Ryland, Jr., December 18, 1809.

[18] Thomas Scott, Letter to John Ryland, Jr., December 18, 1809. When I visited the Haddenham Baptist Church in 2015, the church members related an oral tradition that Thomas Scott wanted his parishioners to attend the Baptist church after he died if a suitable minister could not be found for Aston Sandford. Though this letter to Ryland does not state that Scott *wanted* his people to attend the Baptist church, the attitude he expressed here is certainly consistent with the general character of the oral tradition in Haddenham.

is his relationship with John Ryland Jr.[19] According to Ryland's diary, the two ministers met on October 12, 1779, and they remained firm friends for the rest of their lives.[20] What sets this friendship apart from the others is the fact that a great deal of information can be learned about their interactions through the many extant letters Scott wrote to Ryland.[21] Scott's correspondence with Ryland lasted from at least 1786 to just before the Scott's death in 1821, and their letters were filled with conversations about politics, theology, and other personal matters. The men sent copies of their recent works to one another in order gain feedback and elicit suggestions. They grieved together in their sufferings and rejoiced over each other's successes. For example, Ryland was quick to congratulate Scott for his sermon at the first anniversary meeting of the CMS.[22] He told Scott, "I have just read, and studied your Sermon, and the Design, and Report of the Missionary Society. I have the pleasure to say, the whole has enlightened my Mind, engaged my attention, and moved my affections."[23] Importantly, the entire conversation consistently exhibited all the hallmarks of genuine affection. For instance, Scott signed off a 1786 letter by saying, "We are all tolerably well, and send as much love to you as can be crammed in."[24]

While these quotations convey the general spirit of their friendship, their relationship was not without moments of tension. For instance, several of Scott's letters in the mid-1790s indicate that the two did not always see eye-to-eye on political matters.[25] For example, Ryland was of the opinion, like most

---

[19] This friendship is frequently noted by Ryland's biographers as well. See Christopher W. Crocker, "The Life and Legacy of John Ryland, Jr. (1753–1825): A Man of Considerable Usefulness—An Historical Biography" (PhD dissertation, University of Bristol and Bristol Baptist College, 2018), 337–339; Grant Gordon, "John Ryland. Jr. (1753–1825)," in *The British Particular Baptists 1638-1910,* ed. Michael A.G. Haykin (Springfield, MO: Particular Baptist Press, 2000), 2:86–87.

[20] Jonathan Edwards Ryland, "A Memoir of the Author," in *Pastoral Memorials* (London: B. J. Holdsworth, 1826–1828), 2:36, n.1.

[21] Scott's letters to Ryland have been preserved chiefly in three places. John Scott preserved portions of seven independently dated letters to Ryland (Scott, *Letters and Papers,* 121–142). Parts of several other letters are scattered throughout *The Life of Thomas Scott.* The greatest portion are maintained in the archival holdings of Bristol Baptist College in Bristol, UK.

[22] Thomas Scott, "A Sermon Preached at the Parish Church of St. Andrew by the Wardrobe and St. Anne, Blackfriars, on Tuesday in Whitsun Week, May 26, 1801, before the Society for Missions to Africa and the East," *The Proceedings of the Society for Missions to Africa and the East* (London: Jaques and Co., 1801–1805), 25–74.

[23] John Ryland Jr., Letter to Thomas Scott, July 29, 1801, CMS Archive, CMS/G/AC 3/1/79 (Cadbury Research Library, University of Birmingham, Birmingham, UK).

[24] Thomas Scott, Letter to John Ryland, Jr., May 24, 1786.

[25] See Scott, "Thomas Scott and Evangelical Missions," 156–166.

Dissenters in the eighteenth century, that the Test Act should be abolished because it violated religious liberty by requiring religious tests for holding public office.[26] Scott agreed with Ryland that the Test Act should be repealed, but he insensitively suggested that the Test Act should be viewed as a positive for Dissenters, in that it forced them to trust the Lord and not fall into the temptations associated with participating is civil affairs. He wrote, "If I were a Dissenter, I think I could care less about it; for as a *religious* body the Dissenters will be less led into Temptation, when abridged of their right in this particular, than if freely admitted to places of Trust and profit."[27] What must Ryland have thought of this statement?

But Scott was not the only one to make such a *faux pas* in the course of their friendship. On one occasion, Ryland raised Scott's ire when he passed one of Scott's private letters on to the editor of an American publication called *The Theological Magazine* without obtaining Scott's permission.[28] The letter had been critical of the New Divinity School in New England and specifically targeted the well-known preacher Samuel Hopkins (1721–1803). *The Theological Magazine* ended up publishing Scott's letter, which resulted in him becoming the center of a theological argument in America that he had not initiated nor wanted. When Scott discovered what Ryland had done, he wrote Ryland in frustration, stating that "had [he] entertained the least idea that my thoughts on Hopkins's publications, and on the *Theological Magazine*, were appointed to pass the *ordeal* of American criticism in a public manner, I should certainly have bestowed rather more pains on them."[29] However, Scott seemed to take the whole matter with the good humor afforded dear friends, though he did warn Ryland that he could not "consent to this [June 27, 1797] letter, or any part of it, being sent, as mine, to America," even though he had clarified much of his position with respect to the New Divinity in the letter's contents.[30]

Missteps such as these might have driven lesser men apart, especially given that Scott and Ryland represented two different Christian denominations. Yet, their bond was too deep for such petty matters to divide them, built as it was

---

[26] The Test Act required all persons to make a variety of oaths in order to participate in civic affairs. Included in the Test Act was a requirement that a person must take communion in the Church of England. Dissenters general refused to do so and were therefore barred from public employment. See "First Test Act, 1673," in *English Historical Documents 1660–1714*, ed. Andrew Browning (New York: Oxford University Press, 1953), 389–91.

[27] Thomas Scott, Letter to John Ryland, Jr., December 24, 1792.

[28] The letter Ryland forwarded to the United States remains extant. See Thomas Scott, Letter to John Ryland, Jr., September 22, 1796.

[29] Thomas Scott, Letter to John Ryland, Jr. June 27, 1797.

[30] Thomas Scott, Letter to John Ryland, Jr. June 27, 1797.

on a common faith in the essential doctrines of the gospel. Scott, at least, was "determined, by the help of God, to live and die avowing my cordial reception as a *brother* of every man whom I consider as loving my blessed Lord and Saviour."[31] No doubt, Ryland concurred, and the two carried on their friendship for many years, viewing one another "as brethren in Christ and in the ministry."[32]

The extent of their love for one another could even be seen in how each man approached his respective death. In Scott's case, one of his last letters was directed to Ryland. Scott knew he was dying, and he told Ryland that he did "not expect to continue long."[33] He then, added, "O pray for me, that my faith, hope, love, patience, and fortitude may be increased, and that I may finish my course with joy; for I am apt to be impatient, unbelieving, and cowardly."[34] After a few more pleasantries, he signed the last letter he would ever send to Ryland by saying, "I remain, my dear old friend and fellow labourer, yours faithfully, Thomas Scott."[35] As for Ryland, he was obviously not afforded the opportunity to consult Scott when death approached some four years later. Nevertheless, Scott was, as it were, by Ryland's side. According to his son, Jonathan Edwards Ryland, the elder Ryland "chiefly employed his time, as his debility would allow, in reading, besides the Scriptures, the Life and Remains of the Rev. Thomas Scott, thus refreshing his mind with the memorials of a friendship, which he expected, at no distant interval to renew, and to enjoy forever."[36] It is a testimony to both Scott and Ryland's catholicity that each man was thinking of a friend outside of his own denomination, even at the very end of their lives.

Scott and the Baptist Missionary Society

In light of the friendships that have just been described, it is not altogether surprising that Thomas Scott also had interest in the ministerial endeavors of his Baptist brethren.[37] Importantly, Scott and his friends shared a mutual desire to take the gospel to the ends of the earth. In many ways, the Baptists were forerunners in what came to be known as the "Modern Missions Movement," when they established the BMS in 1792. Yet, other denominations soon followed their

---

[31] Thomas Scott, Letter to John Ryland, Jr. September 4, 1802.

[32] Thomas Scott, Letter to John Ryland, Jr. September 27, 1803.

[33] Thomas Scott, Letter to John Ryland, Jr. February 15, 1821.

[34] Thomas Scott, Letter to John Ryland, Jr. February 15, 1821.

[35] Thomas Scott, Letter to John Ryland, Jr. February 15, 1821.

[36] Jonathan Edwards Ryland, "Memoir of Dr. Ryland," in *Pastoral Memorials: Selected from the Manuscripts of the Late Rev*^{d} *John Ryland, D.D.* (London: B.J. Holdsworth, 1828), 2:35–36.

[37] The majority of this section has been adapted from Scott, "Thomas Scott and Evangelical Missions," 331–335.

lead by forming missionary societies of their own. The London Missionary Society (LMS) was established in 1795 as an inter-denominational agency, and Evangelical Anglicans established the CMS a few years later in 1799. Scott was one of the founding members of the CMS and was elected as its first secretary. The CMS was started as a decidedly Anglican society; and as an Anglican, Scott was naturally more committed and involved in its ministrations. However, the CMS founders desired to maintain good relations with other denominational agencies, and their founding documents called for a "cordial union amongst all Christians, in promoting the common salvation of their Lord and Saviour."[38]

Scott himself personified this catholic attitude, and he aided several other missionary societies in various ways, including the BMS. From the time of its founding onwards, Scott displayed a keen interest in the BMS and followed its progress closely, especially as it related to William Carey's work in India. On April 11, 1798, Scott wrote to Ryland and said, "I rejoice in the accounts of your Missionaries in India. I feel my heart peculiarly knit to Brother Carey; and I have a confidence that, tho' *slowly*, he will *surely* be an instrument of making way for the gospel of Christ in those immense regions."[39] Scott had great respect for Carey; and during a difficult period when the CMS was struggling to find English missionaries, Scott wrote to Ryland to say that "if God should raise us up a [few] *Careys*, all other difficulties would be got over."[40]

From all accounts, Scott believed the BMS to be a model missionary society. In an 1803 letter, he assured Ryland that "you go the right way to work. The word of God translated and dispersed; and attempts to get helpers from the natives."[41] In another letter written later that year, Scott said, "I perhaps approve throughout the proceedings of your Society and of the persons sent forth, more than those of any other Society."[42] Carey's example also provided the inspiration for some of the curriculum of the Aston Sandford seminary, where Scott taught prospective CMS missionaries theology, homiletics, and language skills out of his own home.[43] Even after some of Scott's own students had been labor-

---

[38] "An Account of a Society for Missions to Africa and the East," in *The Proceedings of the Society for Missions to Africa and the East* (London: Jaques and Co., 1801–1805), 1:12.

[39] Thomas Scott, Letter to John Ryland, Jr., April 11, 1798.

[40] Thomas Scott, Letter to John Ryland, Jr., February 1, 1803. Despite being founded in 1799, the CMS did not send its first missionaries to the field until 1804. Even then, the missionaries they sent were from Germany because no English volunteers could be found.

[41] Thomas Scott, Letter to John Ryland, Jr., February 1, 1803.

[42] Thomas Scott, Letter to John Ryland, Jr., December 19, 1803.

[43] Scott had also sought out Ryland's advice on training the missionaries. See Thomas Scott, Letter to John Ryland, Jr., January 8, 1808. In this letter, Scott wrote, "I am now become a tutor of missionaries, and have four Germans, under my care, tho not under my roof. If you can drop me any hints on the subject, I

ing in India for a number of years, Scott poured praise on the BMS:

> I do most heartily rejoice in what your missionaries are doing in India. Their's is the most regular, and best conducted plan against the kingdom of darkness; that modern times has shown; and I augur the most extensive success. More genuine Christian wisdom, fortitude, and disinterested assiduity, perseverance, and patience appear, than I elsewhere read of: May God protect and prosper; May all India be peopled with true Christians; even though they be all Baptists.[44]

These remarks were high praise coming from an Anglican minister who had been involved in the early development of an Anglican missionary society! Accordingly, Scott's hearty approval of the ongoing work of the BMS compelled him to pray regularly for its missionary efforts.

Scott's prayers for the BMS

As stated above, Scott's first priority when it came to missions was the CMS, and the majority of his labor and money went toward advancing its aims. As such, Scott never made a significant material contribution to the BMS. So far as can be determined, he never attended any of the society's functions, nor was he an annual subscriber.[45] However, his lack of regular, pecuniary investment in the BMS should not be understood as a lack of concern for his Baptist brethren. Rather, his involvement simply came in another form, the form of prayer. Scott's correspondence with Ryland makes it clear that Scott prayed regularly for the BMS. In 1803, he told Ryland, "I trust no day passes, but your missionaries are remembered by me."[46] In 1808 he wrote:

> I trust the controversies about missions will have a very good effect. I do not neglect to pray for success to that cause; and to your missionaries particularly, who, I must own, proceed more exactly in the manner, which meets my view of the subject, than any other missionaries, that I shall be obliged to you."

---

[44] Thomas Scott, Letter to John Ryland, Jr., December 3, 1814.

[45] I checked a number of the BMS annual reports, both before and after Scott's involvement with the CMS, and his name does not appear among the list of contributors. When Scott did take up a collection for the Society in 1812, he did not even know where to send the money. See Thomas Scott, Letter to John Ryland, Jr., October 5, 1812. He did, however, make a personal subscription for the expansion of the Baptist Academy in Bristol on at least one occasion. See Thomas Scott, Letter to John Ryland, Jr., April 23, 1807.

[46] Thomas Scott, Letter to John Ryland, Jr., February 1, 1803.

hear of.[47]

Even as his life was drawing to a close, he was still praying for the BMS. In 1819, he wrote to Ryland, "I never miss a day praying for your missionary Society, as well as others; and with an *especially* very often."[48] The affectionate inclusion of the word *especially* in his prayers for the BMS shows just how much Scott loved his Baptist brothers and how much he wished nothing but success for their mission. The nature of these prayers also helps explain why Scott was moved, on at least one occasion, to help the BMS financially.

Scott's Serampore disaster collection
As is common knowledge, William Carey was the first missionary the BMS sent to a foreign field. In 1793, Carey left England for India, where he was to experience over two decades of great hardship in pioneer mission work. Eventually, Carey and his fellow missionaries established a mission in the city of Serampore, India. At the heart of the mission was a printing press that enabled the missionaries to print Bibles and culturally significant books in a variety of languages. After roughly 10 years of work in Serampore, it seemed as if the mission was finally reaching a point of stability. It was then that the unthinkable took place. On March 11, 1812, the BMS print shop caught fire and was severely damaged.[49] Valuable Bible translations, Sanskrit manuscripts, and printing supplies were destroyed. As a result, the BMS sustained an estimated £10,000 in damages.[50] Naturally, morale among the missionaries in Serampore was rather low when Carey sent word back to the BMS about what had taken place.

Word also spread to other Christian groups throughout England; and many, including Thomas Scott, were distraught by the news. Here, once again, we see Scott's catholic spirit come to the fore. When Scott heard "the afflictive news of the calamity," he was moved with compassion for his Baptist brethren, and he told Ryland that he was "determined to address [his] little company on the subject; and to raise a small sum, as a testimony of brotherly sympathy, and cordiality to the cause, in which your honourable *corps* in the east are engaged."[51] In doing so, he hoped that he would "induce others, even in the establishment,

---

[47] Thomas Scott, Letter to John Ryland, Jr., June 20, 1808.

[48] Thomas Scott, Letter to John Ryland, Jr., August 12, 1819.

[49] For an account of the disaster, see Francis Augustus Cox, *History of the Baptist Missionary Society from 1792 to 1842* (London: T. Ward, 1842), 1:213–20. For the context in which the fire took place, see Brian Stanley, *The History of the Baptist Missionary Society 1792-1992* (Edinburgh: T&T Clark, 1992), 36–39.

[50] Cox, *History of the Baptist Missionary Society*, 1:216.

[51] Thomas Scott, Letter to John Ryland, Jr., October 5, 1812.

to do the same, and on a larger scale."[52] As to his own collection he was disappointed at the result of his efforts. He had hoped to raise at least £20, but he "only got £15.16.7."[53] However, he thought Ryland should be encouraged by an expectation of "assistance from every quarter for it is the common cause of Christianity."[54]

Subsequent events proved Scott correct. Christians from all around England rallied in support of the BMS, and the response was so overwhelming that, according to Francis Augustus Cox, "the entire sum required on account of the fire, was raised in the short space of *fifty days*."[55] Cox also recounted hearing Andrew Fuller report to the BMS General Committee that "so constantly are the contributions pouring in from all parties, in and out of the denomination, that I think we must in honesty publish an intimation that the whole deficiency for which we appealed to them is removed."[56] Just how influential Scott had been in garnering some of this support is impossible to determine, but he had been a part of one of the most significant events in BMS history. As Cox has observed, "the greatest advantage [of the Serampore fire] was the powerful impulse given to the mission, by rendering it more generally known, and producing a simultaneous feeling of interest in all denominations."[57]

Conclusion

Two hundred years have now passed since Thomas Scott went home to be with the Lord. Shortly after his death, Scott was buried in the floor of the church at Aston Sandford, and a plaque was placed on a nearby wall, which reads:

> Near this spot are deposited the remains of the Reverend Thomas Scott Twenty years Rector of this Parish. He died April 16th, 1821, aged 74 years. But in his writings he will long remain, and widely proclaim to mankind, The Unsearchable Riches of Christ.[58]

This memorial, while a worthy testimony to Scott, seems in hindsight to

---

[52] Thomas Scott, Letter to John Ryland, Jr., October 5, 1812. Scott was referring to the Church of England when he used the term *establishment* here. His desire was that other Anglicans would also help the BMS.

[53] Thomas Scott, Letter to John Ryland, Jr., October 5, 1812.

[54] Thomas Scott, Letter to John Ryland, Jr., October 5, 1812.

[55] Cox, *History of the Baptist Missionary Society*, 1:220.

[56] Cox, *History of the Baptist Missionary Society*, 1:220.

[57] Cox, *History of the Baptist Missionary Society*, 1:220.

[58] George Libscomb, *The History and Antiquities of the County of Buckingham* (London, 1847), 1:50. The memorial remains there to this day as confirmed by my 2015 visit to Aston Sandford.

be a rather limited statement of his legacy, focusing as it does on his literary achievements. It is true that Scott's "voice" can be heard in his writings, yet Scott deserves to be remembered for much more than what he wrote. Scott was also a pastor, a missionary pioneer, and a friend to all those who put their trust in the gospel of Jesus Christ.

As has been shown in this article, Scott's catholic spirit enabled him to cross denominational lines in order to develop deep friendships with Baptist leaders like Fuller, Carey, and Ryland and to disciple a Baptist pastor in Haddenham. When the opportunity presented itself, he was willing to assist his Baptist brethren recover from a tragedy on the mission field, and he lifted up the BMS repeatedly in his daily prayers. These actions are an important part of Scott's legacy and are an important reminder to modern-day Anglicans and Baptists alike, that the kingdom of God extends far beyond any particular denomination.

The Journal of Andrew Fuller Studies
3 | September 2021

Texts & documents

"Faithful and disinterested friendship": A letter of James Hinton[1]

Introduced and edited by Chance Faulkner

Chance Faulkner serves as a Junior Fellow of the Andrew Fuller Center for Baptist Studies, and is a MTh candidate at Union School of Theology in Wales.

Introduction

The following letter is written to a church member by James Hinton (1761–1823), the minister of the Baptist congregation church in Oxford. A once-ardent Christian has become complacent in his church attendance and has also cut himself off from all communication with Hinton, whose conduct towards him had "uniformly been that of faithful and disinterested friendship." Hinton is using "disinterested" in the classic eighteenth-century usage of "unbiased," or having no hidden agenda. In other words, his is a friendship that seeks his friend's interests above his own. As a tender-hearted shepherd, Hinton is concerned for his spiritual well-being and takes up his pen with deep compassion and pastoral-winsomeness—a trait that marked all of Hinton's ministry and a model for all who shepherd Christ's flock.

---

[1] This letter is found in John Howard Hinton, *A Biographical Portraiture of the late Rev. James Hinton, M.A.* (Oxford: Bartlett and Hinton/London; B.J. Holdsworth, 1824), 213–215. Capitalization has been modernized, and paragraphs divided into shorter lengths.

Text
Dear Sir,
My duty as a minister of Christ is important, and solemn is that charge which enjoins me to watch over souls, as one that must give an account to him who is ready to judge the quick and the dead.[2] To my duty towards my divine Master, I think I may add my Christian affection towards you, as one of the flock over which I am made overseer, as well as a regard to the general prosperity of the Redeemer's interest among us; and by these motives united, I am constrained to address to you a few words of kind inquiry, with respect to your spiritual concerns. In doing this, I act merely as your pastor and friend, and I stand entirely alone.

I read over with pleasure the many expressions of regard which your early letters contain, and feel sorrow that I look in vain for their repetition. Permit me to ask, Have I deserved to be forsaken? Has not my conduct uniformly been that of faithful and disinterested friendship? What then can have caused a withdrawment of your regard? I see with pain your place, as a hearer and as a communicant, almost constantly empty. I look back with mingled pleasure and regret to the interesting autumn of 1797, when (to use your own expressions) "all your attention was arrested by the ministry of the word, and you found it a pleasing task to speak of the goodness of God to you a guilty sinner, and to declare his mercy, that your fellow sinners might fear his holy name." Now, my brother, where is that blessedness you once spake of?[3] Have you not declined from your first love?[4] Do you indeed spend your Lord's days in hearing the precious gospel's joyful sound? Is your soul alive towards God, and in daily enjoyment of communion with him? I am jealous over you with a godly jealousy.[5] You did run well, and you were a companion of them that fear the Lord; but I fear lest by some means the tempter have beguiled you, for we are not ignorant of his devices.[6] As a beloved brother I beseech you to ask, whether you are indeed pursuing a course which will render honour to our divine Master, and secure consolation and prosperity in your own soul? With joy I saw you begin your Christian race: the world and Satan beheld the sight with grief and displeasure. But oh! are not both the joy and grief likely to be transferred? Are you sure that you are not drinking again into the spirit of the world? I beseech you to pray earnestly over these inquiries, and carefully to examine your own

---

[2] 1 Peter 4:5.

[3] Galatians 4:15.

[4] Revelation 2:4.

[5] 2 Corinthians 11:2.

[6] 2 Corinthians 2:11.

heart and conduct. Most truly glad shall I be to find the result all that you or I can wish; but if it be not, there is a voice (O may it speak with power!) which says "Return unto me, ye backsliding children; I will heal your backslidings, I will love you freely."[7]

I beg to say one word respecting your duties as a church member. I put the church covenant into your hands previously to your union with us: you said you approved, and you requested to be admitted. Will you have the goodness to look at the solemn, the voluntary engagement to which, you requested your name might be added? It runs thus: "We do conscientiously promise, nothing extraordinary preventing, to meet together at all appointed seasons at the Lord's table, and on all other opportunities."[8] Surely here are no unscriptural requirements: less than this can never hold a Christian society together. But have you observed these duties? Suppose you could walk more happily with any other Christian society; surely you should regard the Lord's commands to walk in his ordinances, and to cultivate the unity of the Spirit, and the fellowship of the saints. I can say from my heart I have not a selfish wish: rejoicing in the delightful hope that God graciously employed me to snatch you as a brand out of the fire,[9] I shall equally rejoice to see you an ornament of any church under heaven, and would gladly lend my aid for this purpose. My Christian regard would not flag for a moment. Do not then believe that I have more than this one wish respecting you: May you walk with God! May you adorn his doctrine! May you have a conscience truly tender, yet void of offence towards God and towards man! Convince me that this is the case, and my anxiety will be immediately turned into joy, and my admonitions into congratulation.

---

[7] Jeremiah 3:22.

[8] For the full church covenant see "The Church Covenant of 1780," http://newroad.org.uk/wp-content/uploads/2017/06/NRBC-Covenant.pdf (accessed April 6, 2021). See also Paul S. Fiddes, "Receiving One Another: The History and Theology of the Church Covenant, 1780," in *A Protestant Catholic Church of Christ: Essays on the History and Life of New Road Baptist Church, Oxford*, ed. Rosie Chadwick (Oxford, UK: New Road Baptist Church, 2003), 65–105.

[9] Jude 1:23.

"...With politics I never meddle, though my heart cannot be indifferent to the happiness of man": A letter of James Hinton on religious liberty

Introduced and edited by Chance Faulkner

Chance Faulker serves as a Junior Fellow of the Andrew Fuller Center for Baptist Studies, and is a MTh candidate at Union School of Theology in Wales.

Introduction

In 1800, Michael Angelo Taylor (1757–1834), MP for Poole, sought to put forward a motion in the English legislature to amend the Act of Toleration (1688) and require dissenting ministers to be licensed for itinerate preaching. This meant that gospel preachers would be required to adhere to government guidelines and interference in pulpit ministry. The following letter is from Oxford pastor, James Hinton (1761–1823), to William Smith (1756–1835), MP for Sudbury,[1] requesting that he defend the Dissenters and plead with Taylor to

[1] William Smith was an abolitionist known for fighting for human rights, including religious freedom, and was said to be "at the center of every good cause of his day" (Esther J. Evans and John Lawrence Sharpe, eds., *Gnomon: Essays for the Dedication of the William R. Perkins Library, April 16, 1970* [Durham: Duke University Library, 1970], 28). Smith was also the first Unitarian English Politician (Philip Gaskell, *Morvern Transformed: A Highland Parish in the Nineteenth Century* [Cambridge; New York; Melbourne: Cambridge University Press, 1980], 57). See also Gareth Atkins, *Converting Britannia: Evangelicals and British Public*

cease from moving forward with the motion.

As a minister of the gospel, Hinton sought to stay out of politics. Nevertheless, the proposed motion would certainly cause a fresh attack on itinerant preachers and have significant spiritual consequences on those under his care. "With politics, I never meddle," Hinton says, but "my heart cannot be indifferent to the happiness of man," and so he takes up his pen in mediation. One thing that stands out in this letter is Hinton's calm, gentle, courteous, yet confident and firm rhetoric. He is a model of what it looks like to be firm in one's convictions while obeying the New Testaments imperative "to be obedient, to be ready for every good work, to speak evil of no one, to avoid quarreling, to be gentle, and to show perfect courtesy toward all people" (Titus 3:1–2).

Text
James Hinton, Letter to William Smith, Esq. M.P., 1800 [2]

Sir,
I learn from the papers that Mr. M.A. Taylor intends a motion respecting dissenters, or rather dissenting ministers.[3] I cannot judge precisely of his object, but it seems to be some limitation of the act (19. Geo. III.)[4] respecting the registry of preachers. I have full confidence that you, sir, as one of our public guardians, will carefully watch every attempt to abridge our religious privileges: with politics I never meddle, though my heart cannot be indifferent to the happiness of man. Very few, if any, of the evils which the proposed enactments would cure, actually exist; while their introduction would create very serious mischiefs. One instance I will give, and it is similar to a thousand others. I preach, perhaps once a month, at a village, six miles from any meeting-house. On a Sunday, in bad weather, the families who live there, all poor, are happy enough to find one person able to read intelligibly to the rest; or perhaps a young man, taking Dr. Watts's[5] Sermons in his pocket, walks from Oxford, reads to them, prays with them, and returns. This is a truly Christian charity to

---

Life, 1770–1840 (Woodbridge, Suffolk: Boydell Press, 2019), 22.

[2] This letter is from John Howard Hinton, *A Biographical Portraiture of the late Rev. James Hinton, M.A.* (Oxford: Bartlett and Hinton; London: B.J. Holdsworth, 1824), 355–356. Capitalization has been modernized.

[3] See Jennifer Mori, *Britain in the Age of the French Revolution: 1785–1820* (London; New York; Routledge, 2014), 117–118.

[4] The Nonconformist Relief Act of 1779 allowed for dissenting ministers to preach and serve in England provided they pledge allegiance to the crown and confess to the Scriptures as their final authority.

[5] Isaac Watts (1674–1748) was a hymn writer, logician, and congregationalist minister of Mark Lane Congregational in London.

the poor and the ignorant, the aged and the infirm; but such are the prejudices excited against us, that nothing can screen such a young man from all the horrid penalties of the [A]ct of [U]niformity,[6] but a legal register; for he acts as the conductor of public worship in a congregation exceeding five persons. It is not merely the insolence of the mob we fear, though that (as you know) is dreadful enough in Oxfordshire.[7] I know an instance in this county, in a Presbyterian congregation, where the people were threatened by the clergyman, for meeting to read and pray while their minister was ill. Our friends never resort to the privilege of registering themselves without necessity, nor even plead it as a bar to militia laws, &c.; and for those who are inimical to us to know that we could not recur to this protection would do us much injury. We are often examined very closely by magistrates, and forced to conform to the laws in every iota; nor would the highest respectability of character or talents, unprotected by positive and express law, weigh aught against the dreadful charges of disaffection and schism. The [T]oleration [A]ct,[8] and that above mentioned, founded on it, are our only bulwarks; and I deeply regret that such a man as Mr. T[aylor] should, at such a time, bring forward a motion, which may serve as a signal for a fresh attack on a body of respectable men, whom he knows to have been unworthily treated. Our ecclesiastical justices of the peace (and we have almost all such) would very much like to have some discretionary power in this business (which I trust they never will have) and it is with reluctance that they execute the present laws. Even county courts sometimes refuse to register very respectable ministers and places, and are obliged to comply by threats of a mandamus.

---

[6] The Act of Uniformity (1549, 1552, 1559, 1662) was an English Parliament Act which sought to unify the church by mandating that all religious services be structured around the *Book of Common Prayer*. Those who refused to conform were either fined, imprisoned, revoked, or expelled.

[7] Hinton knows of the insolence of the mob at first-hand. Six years earlier, in 1794, a large armed mob broke up the service he was leading in Woodstock. Hinton and his three companions were violented attacked and barely escaped with their lives. See Hinton, *A Biographical Portraiture*, 255–265; Michael A.G. Haykin, "James Hinton of Oxford: A biographical sketch," in *The Diary of James Hinton (1761–1823)*, ed. Chance Faulkner (Peterborough, ON: H&E Publishing, 2020), 13–14. According to Joseph Ivimey (1773–1834), Hinton, who was the Baptist minister in Oxford, was "called to fill perhaps one of the most difficult stations in which a nonconformist minister, in England, could have been placed" (Joseph Ivimey, *The excellence and utility of an evangelical ministry, as exercised by Protestant Dissenters* [London: John Offor, 1823], A2).

[8] The Toleration Act of 1689 was an English Parliament Act that allowed for dissenting (Non-Conformist) ministers freedom to worship in their chapels with the protection of the law under certain condition. Dissenting chapels were obligated to be licensed, pay tithes to the Church of England for the chapels' maintenance and upkeep, and contribute to the clergy's salaries. If a member of a dissenting church wished to be legally married, they had to be married by an Anglican minister in an Anglican church. Ministers had to subscribe to the Thirty-Nine Articles of Religion (with the exemption of four) and take an oath of allegiance. They were also required to reject the Roman Catholic doctrine of transubstantiation. Dissenters were also generally restricted from civil service, politics, and attending the university. Still, some exceptions were granted if they agreed to receive the Sacraments administered by the Church of England.

I value Mr. T[aylor] as I trust he is a friend to liberty and to man; and if you, sir, are personally acquainted with him, I hope it will not be difficult to convince him that, however some hot headed youth of seventeen may have misbehaved, it would be unjust, on that account, to subject to galling chains a great number of his fellow citizens, heartily attached to the constitution and the real interests of their country.

A letter of Thomas Davis on his conversion[1]

Introduced and edited by Michael A.G. Haykin

Michael A.G. Haykin is Chair and Professor of Church History and Director, The Andrew Fuller Center for Baptist Studies at The Southern Baptist Theological Seminary, Louisville, Kentucky.

Introduction

It is not at all surprising that, in the study of evangelical Christianity during the long eighteenth century, the remarkable ministries of men like George Whitefield or the Wesley brothers that spanned continents and created denominations have been well researched. Yet, there are other stories, no less thrilling, that are worth retrieving from this paradigmatic age of revival. One of them is the renewal of the Particular Baptist cause at Reading under the ministry of Thomas Davis (1734–1796), whom I would venture to guess is an almost complete unknown today.[2] Certainly one reason for this obscurity is the fact that apart from a confession of faith delivered at his ordination, there appears to be virtually nothing extant from Davis' pen. In an account of Davis' life, John Rippon (1751–1836) includes a few extracts of his letters and informs his readers

---

[1] "Letter of the late Mr. Davies [sic], of Reading," *The Baptist Magazine* 3 (1811): 239–242.

[2] For details of Thomas Davis' life, I am indebted to John Rippon, "The Rev. Thomas Davis, Reading, Berks," in his *The Baptist Annual Register, for 1794, 1795, 1796-1797* (London, 1797), 514–523, and Ernest A. Payne, *The Baptists of Berkshire Through Three Centuries* (London: Carey Kingsgate Press, 1951), 90–91.

that Davis was wont to write out many of his sermons in full. But sadly, none of the latter are extant.[3] What follows is the longest extant letter of Davis. It related his evangelical conversion.

Text
Dear and honoured brother,   Reading, September 1769

I can but with gratitude acknowledge your kindness to unworthy me, in giving yourself the trouble to write to one who is not worthy the notice of any of God's people. I am not meet to be called your brother in so sacred a character as you sustain as a minister of Jesus Christ: because I am as one born out of due time, and so lately a persecutor of the Church of Christ. But it is by the grace of God I am what I am, and I would humbly hope that his grace has not been bestowed on me in vain. Were I to relate to you somewhat of the goodness of God to my soul, you would conclude that I am a monument of sparing mercy, an object of everlasting love, and a subject of distinguishing and sovereign grace. I may say that I am the seed of believing parents. My family has been highly favoured of God and is so to this day. But I am not going to tell you that I was (as some say) brought into the covenant this way, nor by being sprinkled in my infancy; but by an act of sovereign grace from eternity. What I have an eye to, in saying my parents were believers, is to let you see how deep my crimes have been against God, after such godly advice and good example.

My father is gone to glory upwards of 30 years; my mother has been baptized upwards of 40 years; she is justly called a mother in Israel. She has alive ten sons and daughters, who have, I trust, *all* tasted that the Lord is gracious; she has lately lost a brother who has been deacon of a Baptist church some years, and often exercised in the pulpit. She has now living a sister, a gracious good woman, and two nephews and one niece called by grace; they are all Baptists and members of churches. I have a brother a Baptist minister, another brother I expect soon to be called to that work, and one of my cousins before mentioned is now exercising his talents. Yet our family was poor in Manasseh, and I can say I was the least and most vile of all my father's house. Thus you see, my dear friend, the amazing grace of God to my unworthy family. But what is more wonderful to me is that I should be a part of those happy few (after all my uncommon rebellion) to whom it is our Father's good pleasure to give the kingdom.

My parents began to train me up for God, but I went astray from the womb speaking lies. By the time was twelve years of age, I was a thief, a most wretched

---
[3] Rippon, "Rev. Thomas Davis," 517.

liar, and a horrid sinner. It was expected by most that knew me that I should finish my course upon the gallows, and it was an amazing providence that appeared for me, or it had been my fatal case. These things brought my dear parents into deep distress and woe. But the impression soon wore off my mind, and shortly after I went 10miles distant from my parents, apprentice to a bricklayer, where with desire I learned to swear, though often to the wounding of my conscience, not being used to such a practice while among my friends. But here God granted me my desire in a most awful manner, for few ever went such lengths as I was given up to. I served about two years of my apprenticeship and then left my master. Now I got to be a smuggler, living in a sea-port town, and then wandering about the country for about 2 years, cheating all I could. After this I found a companion, and we started for London, where I worked at my calling about two years more, living in all manner of sin and immorality. I was obliged to quit this place, and seek for a new situation, where I worked a year and got married into a sober family. But this made no difference in me. I went on, after that, for three years, swearing, drinking, and in every evil work, till God was pleased to stop me, as the proud waves, saying, "hitherto shalt thou go, and no farther."

I happened to go out of curiosity, with some more like me, to hear what we called Methodist preaching, but it was a Baptist minister. He took his text from Luke 12, "Cut it down, why cumbereth it the ground? Spare it this year also." This was the awful time that God was gracious to such a wretched sinner. A time never to be forgotten. Whilst Justice was lifting up the axe, Mercy stepped in. Thus this brand was plucked from the burning. The change was great, sudden, and amazing to the whole town and more so, abundantly more so, to myself. In about 4 years after, I was called to preach that faith which I once destroyed, and that in the face my of old companions. This brought upon me much persecution, even to the loss of my bread, and all my pretended friends. My trials now became very many and very great.

But I had not preached long before I had many invitations in London and in the Country, occasioned by the great desire many had to see the furious lion now become a lamb. I had not exercised but about four months, before I was called to Reading. I must say it was of God, but time and paper would fail to tell you how astonishingly it was brought about. However, here I was sent, to a drooping, dying cause, and having obtained help God of, I continue to this day, in spite of all the opposition I meet with from the world and the devil. I have been here about two years and four months, and I trust the Lord has made me useful as the clay to open many blind eyes. I have baptized 56, and such as I have reason to believe have received the grace of God in truth. They all behave as becometh the Gospel, except one. I think to baptize 4 more next month. The Lord is carrying on a great work at Reading. My labour is hard, but blessed be

God it is pleasant, having much of the presence of God. As I have laboured hard in doing the Devil's drudgery, I desire now to spend and be spent for God's glory and the love I bear to precious souls, knowing, if I should hold my peace, the very stones must cry out.

Book Reviews

Michael A.G. Haykin and Paul M. Smalley, eds., *Puritan Piety: Writings in Honor of Joel R. Beeke* (Fearn, Ross-shire: Mentor, 2018), 296 pages.

A glance at the chronological bibliography of Joel Beeke's writings (pp. 271–296) explains why editors Michael A.G. Haykin and Paul M. Smalley chose to entitle this collection of essays in Beeke's honor *Puritan Piety*. Beeke's nearly forty years of scholarship has thoroughly demonstrated that biblical piety is at the heart of Puritan theology. In Beeke's writings, one will immediately notice that he consistently combines rigorous scholarship with a pastoral tone and an eye towards spiritual transformation. As Smalley helpfully notes, "Like Calvin before him, Joel Beeke prioritizes piety as the aim of all Christian doctrine and effort" (p. 14). The essays in this collection also demonstrate the priority of piety.

Divided into four parts, each part of this collection connects various aspects of Puritan thought to Puritan piety. Part one explores the Reformed theology on which Puritan piety rests. Part two explores Puritan piety as it relates to the means of grace. Part three provides "individual snapshots of Puritan piety." Part four introduces us to two later heirs of Puritan piety. The focus of these essays is not to explore Puritan piety as it appears in the writings of Beeke, but to explore the ardent piety of Reformers such as Calvin and the English Puritans. In his own way, each author, whether exploring John Cotton's theology of psalm-singing (W. Robert Godfrey), John Owen's view of the Lord's Supper (Sinclair B. Ferguson), or Thomas Manton's preaching on Psalm 119 (J. Stephen Yuille), demonstrates the centrality of holy scripture in Puritan piety. The work of the Spirit, which is essential to Puritan piety, is always tethered to the Bible. This overarching theme is woven throughout the book.

Of particular interest to those who admire Andrew Fuller is Michael Haykin's essay on Fuller's pneumatology as it relates to a minister's usefulness. Haykin, following B.B. Warfield and others, maintains that Puritan piety centered upon biblical pneumatology. Such was the case for Puritan heirs, among whom Haykin numbers Andrew Fuller. Haykin writes: "[T]he Puritans and their heirs—that is, the Calvinistic Baptists, Presbyterians, and Congregationalists—were men and women whose ultimate ardency was about the Christian experience of the Holy Spirit" (p. 255). Yet Fuller, like the Puritans, did not believe the Christian's experience of the Holy Spirit was wholly mystical—it was rooted in one's study of the Bible and a devotion to sincere prayer (pp. 261–265). In turn, the Spirit's work through these means of grace enabled the minister to be eminently useful for the Lord's service. Fuller clearly echoed the teachings of the Puritans.

Puritan Piety is a valuable resource for exploring the Puritan understanding of biblical holiness. Each essay in this volume makes a valuable contribution to the field of Puritan studies, but each essay also leads the reader to consider more deeply the grace and love of God in Jesus Christ, which is at the heart of Puritan piety.

Jesse F. Owens
Assistant Professor of Historical and Systematic Theology
Welch College, Gallatin, TN

William H. Brackney, and Evan L. Colford, eds., *Come Out From Among Them, and Be Ye Separate, Saith the Lord: Separation and the Believer's Church Tradition* (Eugene, OR: Pickwick, 2019), xix + 235 pages.

A common question raised among new Christians is "Why are there so many different churches or denominations?" If there is only one Lord and one faith, then why all the unique groups, widely differing in theological sensibilities, all claiming to be Christian and many claiming to be the one and only true path to God? This collection of essays from the seventeenth Believer's Church Conference held at Acadia Divinity School in Wolfville, Nova Scotia in 2016 goes a long way to answering this question.

As a collection of essays these contributions are both spot on and wide of the proposed mark. Some essays are laser-focused and provide excellent insights into the stated conference theme: "The Tendency Toward Separation. Come-Outers among the Believer Churches: Historical Realities and Ecclesial Concerns Among Dissenter Traditions." For example, William Brackney's excellent essay (Ch. 2 "The Genetic Separatist Trait Among the Baptists") delineates Baptist separatist varieties in a most insightful way. Baptists, "a leading category of the Free Church movement" (p. 23) and an historically separatist movement emerging from English Puritan separatism, has no less than five categories of come-outer movements. Those driven by theology (the General and Particulars in English Baptist history); ethical and racial (black Baptist movements post-Civil War); reformist movements (anti-slavery groups); issues of polity (Landmarkism); and *prima donnas* (groups loyal to men, e.g. Thomas Todhunter Shields, Canadian fundamentalist). Brackney's taxonomy of Baptist come-outer groups provides real understanding to someone unfamiliar with the Baptist landscape. Baptists, birthed in separatism, had no problem sundering existing fellowships when the stakes were too high to maintain unity.

The same could be said of Douglas A. Foster's chapter (Ch. 4 "Unifiers to Come-Outers") on the Stone-Campbell Movement, ironically a movement birthed to oppose Christian group splinting. Soon the SCM become a fractious movement itself. Progenitors Barton Stone and the Campbells, Alexander and his father Thomas, envisioned movements of simple Bible people but soon found out that internal conflicts arose for some of the same kinds of reasons Brackney described among the Baptists two chapters earlier. David Emmanuel Goatley's chapter (Ch. 7 "Making Room to Serve") highlights the fragmentation among African-American Baptists.

On the opposite end are several essays that, while excellent in themselves, seem out of place given the stated title of the conference. Eileen Barker's chapter (Ch. 10 "The Curse of Cults and the Scourge of Sects: Or a Coming-Out of New Religious Movements") is a survey of a wide assortment of quasi-biblical to non-biblical religious movements of relatively recent vintage. A sampling of groups covered include World-wide Church of God, the Jehovah's Witnesses and the Mormons (quasi-biblical) to Hindu and Islamic movements that have no part in Christianity, much less in a "Believer's Church" tradition. Her essay is an interesting survey of these groups but it really does not advance the purpose of the book as there is little real "Believer's Church" thinking among these groups.

A second fascinating but divergent essay is Karen Smith's essay (Ch. 6 "Holy Living and Holy Dying:" The Responses of Some British Baptist Women to 'Come-Out' from the World'"). Like the previous essay, this one is well-written, but it seems tangential to the over-all conference theme, focusing solely of British Baptist women and their separation from the world rather from their fellows.

Come Out From Among Them is a most helpful survey in the broad contours of what it tries to accomplish. These essays examine the great diversity of "Believer Church" traditions and shows why many preferred fragmentation to ecumenicity. Preservation of distinctives, sometimes theological, at other times social or otherwise, drove believers apart rather than drew them together. The things held in common were less important than the things held uniquely. Whether judged right or wrong among humanity or the rest of the Church, these groups felt that certain commitments required the sundering of relationships rather than the compromise of cooperation.

It seems likely that Jesus' prayer for unity (John 17:21) will not be realized in this life but only in the next. The only thing we can *all* agree on is that there are many things we *don't* agree on. Therein lies the problem. Even so, come Lord Jesus.

Jeff Straub, PhD
Independent scholar

Michael A.G. Haykin, *Eighteenth-Century Evangelicals as Spiritual Mentors*, The Christian Mentor, Volume 3 (Kitchener, ON: Joshua Press, 2018), 210 pages.

It would not be difficult to argue that perhaps one of the most misunderstood terms in the Western world today—whether in Christian circles or broader society—is "evangelical." With some wanting to abandon the term altogether, Michael A.G. Haykin has provided a work that seeks to rekindle a love for what "evangelical" originally communicated by examining the rich, deep-rooted spirituality of the evangelical movement.

In the third volume of The Christian Mentor series, Michael A.G. Haykin brings together a collection of "key aspects," such as "the anointed preaching, the new birth and justification, the Lord's Supper, hymnody and spiritual direction" (pp. 7–8) by surveying leading figures of "the eighteenth-century evangelical revival," which "began in the 1730s and found its centre in the English-speaking world on both sides of the Atlantic" (pp. 6–7).

Haykin informs the reader that "all of these studies are grounded upon a deep-seated conviction that the eighteenth-century is the most important Christian era along with those of the fourth and sixth centuries, which witnessed the hammering out of Nicene Trinitarian orthodoxy and the Reformation respectively" (p. 8). Putting his cards on the table, Haykin concurs with D. Martyn Lloyd-Jones (1899–1981) in affirming, "I am an eighteenth-century man" (p. 8). For this reason, Haykin's desire for the reader is to see that "our great need is for an outpouring of the Spirit that unfurls the love of God in the depth and to the extent that our eighteenth-century forebears knew" (p. 8).

After introducing the reader to the overall moral and ecclesial depravity of English life at the end of the seventeenth century, Haykin then presents the persons through whom this great revival came to such a barren people. These persons, presented respectively in chapters 2 through 9, include, George Whitefield, Charles Wesley, William Williams, William Grimshaw, John Newton, Anne Dutton, Andrew Fuller, and William Carey. The final chapter "deals primarily with a topic rather than one individual, namely, the issue of the gifts of the Spirit" (p. 8), a subject which has received a significant amount of attention among Christians in recent years.

Presenting George Whitefield as being the one "who, more than any other figure, epitomized" the eighteenth-century evangelical revival in Great Britain (p. 7) may come as a surprise to some. However, the choice of Whitefield to begin the book, as a foundational figure, is strategic, for "just as [Martin] Luther's conversion was the spark that lit the fires of the Reformation, so Whitefield's conversion would be central to kindling the blaze of the eighteenth-century evangelical revival" (p. 14). Haykin reasons that Whitefield should be seen as the true leader of the eighteenth-century revival. Haykin argues that Whitefield's (not Wesley's) innovation of open-air preaching was "a key turning-point … in the history of evangelicalism" (p. 17). With his Reformation and Puritan-rooted theology, Whitefield's extensive itinerant ministry caused widespread influence on both sides of the Atlantic.

What may be most surprising to the reader is not *what* Haykin left out in his dedicated character studies, but *who*. Most apparent in the omissions are John Wesley and Jonathan Edwards. While both men do make an appearance at points in the book—Wesley most notably in the chapter on Whitefield and Edwards in the final chapter dealing with the subject of the Holy Spirit in revival—their absence in the table of contents, as main characters, may cause some to scratch their heads.

On the other hand, among those receiving individual chapters may very well be figures who are unfamiliar to most readers, which helps to set this book apart from others written on key figures during this period. In addition, Haykin's bountiful inclusion of contemporary persons within each chapter introduces the reader to far more than the table of contents would let on. Therefore, what potentially serves as one of the book's greatest weaknesses of may very well be considered its greatest strength.

Haykin's Baptist heritage and *forte* are apparent, without being overbearing, in this work. This is evident in many instances, such as Grimshaw's influence upon the Particular Baptists in Yorkshire (pp. 77–79); Newton's appeal to William Wilberforce on Carey's behalf (pp. 88–90), his involvement in mentoring John Ryland, Jr. (pp. 91–97), and his comforting counsel to the bereaved Sarah Pearce (pp. 97–99); entire chapters devoted to Dutton, Fuller, and Carey; the appearance of Benjamin Beddome and John Gill in Dutton's chapter; and finally, the inclusion of the Calvinistic Baptists, most notably Ryland in the final chapter on the operation of the Spirit in revival.

This work is commendable to any student of church history, whether in the academy of in the pew. Haykin's writing is easily accessible and engaging. May Haykin's goal in writing this work be achieved, and may we adopt these friends from the past as spiritual mentors.

Jordan A. Senécal
Library and Learning Centre Director
Heritage College and Seminary, Cambridge, ON

David W. Bebbington, *Baptists Through the Centuries: A History of a Global People*, 2nd edition (Waco, TX: Baylor University Press, 2018), 383 pages.

Though the history of the Baptist movement has been catalogued in numerous works, David Bebbington's work is one that is both concise, yet insightful, providing an engaging overview of Baptists and their contributions to worldwide Christianity. Bebbington understands that Baptists do not possess a monolithic identity, nor are they concentrated in one area of the world (though they have for most of their history resided in Britain and North America). Bebbington doesn't deal with every place where Baptist thought and experience has been found, rather his goal is to "discuss broad trends with representative instances" (p. 4). Hence, this book serves the purpose of providing an excellent and compelling summary of the global movement of Baptist faith and practice.

Bebbington begins his discussion in the Reformation, where the origins of the Baptist movement lie. Baptists were influenced by all the major continental Reformers including Luther, Zwingli, and Calvin. Though influential, as Bebbington notes, the actual Baptist traditions "were to emerge from developments in England" (p. 13). The Lollard movement inspired by John Wyclif seeded the growing dissent which had affinities with the later continental reformations. Bebbington traces this thought to the later Puritan movement of the late 16th century, which then gave way to separatism and the emergence of Baptist congregations. These early congregations where "preoccupied with ensuring that they should flee from all residual trances of Catholic influence" (p. 22) within the Church of England, especially those practices re-introduced by Archbishop Laud (1573–1645). Baptists were "products of their time" and represented the influences from the Reformation, Puritanism, and separatism. Inconclusive, however, is the influence of Anabaptism upon Baptists. At most, notes Bebbington, General Baptists "seem to have accepted the doctrine of general redemption" from Anabaptists (p. 41).

Bebbington captures the dynamic between Particular and General Baptists in seventeenth-century England, noting their theological distinctions while also recognizing their common commitments to converted church membership and believer's baptism. There was even some flexibility between the two groups in accepting members from one another, as well as instances where solidarity existed as fellow Dissenters. Bebbington aptly covers Baptist participation in the revivals of the eighteenth century, which led to an increased desire for evangelism and world missions, particularly under William Carey, the father of modern missions. Though revival brought renewed spiritual activity and action, it eventually led to division in the subsequent century. Bebbington relates: "Strong-minded souls who confidently carved out their own path in religion threatened the unity of denominational structures" (p. 85). Further discussion of divisions within Baptist thought and practice are represented in chapters 7, 8, and 9 dealing with topics such as the social gospel and race among Baptists, particularly in the 20th century.

With these and the following chapters, Bebbington covers various individual topics related to Baptist life and thought. "Women in Baptist life" is the subject of chapter 10, wherein the undeniable contributions of women are rightly noted. Bebbington remarks, "Whether philanthropy was a matter of organized societies, money raising, or simply visiting, women took the lead" (p. 166). There was a fervent spirit of religious activity among Baptist women, especially in the areas of missions, spirituality, and social endeavors. Church ministry (chapter 11), religious liberty (chapter 12), and foreign missions (chapter 13) all receive a concise historical treatment in these latter chapters. The final chapters of Bebbington's text relate the global spread and influence of Baptist thought and practice. Baptists truly are a global people, perpetuated by the ongoing mission and church planting efforts. Accordingly, Baptist growth also occurred through opposition and oppression (p. 243–5). Such oppression did not extinguish Baptists but often led to their flourishing, also aided by "international action in favor of religious liberty" (p. 244). Thus the "global spread of the Baptists … was therefore a more complex process than is sometimes suggested" (p. 248). Bebbington also attests to how Baptist life and thought is well represented in places such as Latin America, Nigeria, and in North-East Asia. Concluding the text is a chapter on Baptist identity providing a summative view of how Baptists have perceived themselves theologically and culturally, focusing primarily on the twentieth and twenty-first century.

This text is an excellent history of the Baptist movement and is one of the most approachable texts of its kind. Bebbington has done an excellent job in highlighting the global nature of the Baptist movement, as indicated in the title. The work is summative in nature, so many topics deserve much greater consideration. To this end, Bebbington offers a list of texts for further reading at the end of each chapter. The work is well-researched and demonstrative of an author who knows his subject well. He has done a superb job in not only cataloging the Baptist movement but giving it leverage for the next generation of historians and Baptist scholars. Should you read one text on the history of the Baptists, choose this one.

Coleman M. Ford
Assistant Professor of Christian Formation
Director of Professional Doctoral Studies
Southwestern Baptist Theological Seminary

Tom Nettles, *Easier for a Camel: Andrew Fuller's View of Man's Absolute Dependence on Grace* (Conway, AR: Free Grace Press, 2019), 100 pages.

The last few decades have seen an increased interest in the "indefatigable and fearless" Andrew Fuller (p. 16), a "key thinker among the Particular Baptists of England" (p. 41). As pastors and scholars have been encountering Fuller, they have been realizing the importance of his works and the multifaceted, timeless wisdom with which he preached and wrote, helping to bring revival to his contemporary Calvinistic Baptists. Fuller has much to teach us, for "he gave a brilliant theological rationale for the beginning of the modern missions movement, rallied Baptists and evangelicals in England and America for the support of the missionary society, and propagated a robust doctrinal orthodoxy through his polemical, apologetic, and theological writings" (p. 41). His thought became known, even in his day, as "Fullerism" (p. 17).

Tom Nettles, in *Easier for a Camel*, has succinctly arranged Fuller's "defenses of Calvinism" from "among his theological and polemical writings" (p. 41). Originally written as "short *ad hoc* articles" produced in response to "erroneous presentations of Fuller's views" on "God's saving grace," they have been compiled into this nine-chapter work, with some slight reworking to "create a sense of coherence and continuity in the overall arrangement" (p. 12). Nettles' desire is "that any who read it may find it helpful in advancing their understanding of Andrew Fuller and his importance as a devoted steward of the manifold grace of God" (p. 13).

While Nettles is not exactly clear on what the source of these erroneous views are, the reader can begin to see, as a recurring theme throughout the book, that Nettles is responding to a controversy within the Southern Baptist

Convention over the doctrines of grace (otherwise known as "Calvinism")—as put forward by the "Traditional Baptists" in their 2012 *Statement of the Traditional Southern Baptist Understanding of God's Plan of Salvation* (pp. 39, 89). Nettles states that the "late-eighteenth-century controversy duplicates many of the issues currently under discussion as matters of difference among Southern Baptists" and that he sees the current controversy as being "a renewal of the discussion between the non-Calvinist Baptist Dan Taylor and the Calvinist Baptist Andrew Fuller" (p. 46). The chapters themselves do a wonderful job in presenting Fuller within his own context, and the resulting application to this controversy only appears in brief remarks, often in the concluding paragraph (pp. 32, 38, 46, 53, 60–61, 89–93).

Nettles' work, while being short, is dense and will require the reader to be focused on the carefully selected and pointed argumentation contained within. In this work, he follows some of Fuller's interaction with, and response to, the errors of Socinianism, Sandemanianism, Arminianism, and in some instances, High Calvinism. Nettles points out that Fuller "identified Arminianism as one step on the journey from robust Christianity toward eventual infidelity" (p. 28). Tracing this progression, he noted that it is not common for "persons who go over to Socinianism, to go directly from Calvinism, but through one or other different stages of Arminianism, or Arianism, or both" (p. 32). For this reason, Nettles understands the current controversy to be an important one in avoiding the slippery slope into greater error, which includes Open Theism (p. 32).

The first two chapters examine some "rules of engagement" from the "master Baptist controversialist" (pp. 19–20) as well as some convictions that led Fuller to engage in controversial matters. These chapters will prove to be helpful, especially in a day and age of constant (and instant) interaction, often involving controversial matters. Principled engagement is necessary.

Much of the book is devoted to Fuller's interactions with Dan Taylor, "the leading light among the English New Connection General Baptists" (p. 42). In so doing, Nettles presents various defenses of Calvinism that Fuller put forward in his writings, namely on the issues of human inability and responsibility, the freedom (or bondage) of the will, election, the relationship between regeneration and faith, the nature of saving faith, irresistible grace, definite (or limited) atonement, the free offer of the gospel, and perseverance.

One major strength of the book is how Nettles models the principle of *ad fontes* by filling the book with primary source quotations. In reading this work, the reader will be receiving a crash course in the Calvinistic theology of Andrew Fuller.

The only notable chapter where Nettles' voice is dominant is in chapter 8, however, even then he is mostly examining the biblical data on the nature of the atonement—the reality of Christ's dying both for *sin* (general) as well as *sins* (specific). This chapter, as well as the one that precedes it, will prove to be a helpful contribution to the debate surrounding Fuller's view of the atonement.

Given that the book is a collection of articles, it could have benefitted from more effort in organizing and synthesizing the material. For example, persons and works who appear without much comment in earlier parts of the book receive more complete or detailed introductions in later parts when those works or persons are brought up again. Likewise, the repetition of material was noticeable, however it was not unbearable. The book could have also been aided by a more robust introduction wherein the context of the chapters would have been more clearly presented, preparing the understanding of the reader before diving headlong into the material.

Despite these shortcomings, this work is commendable. However, it may be best served by those who are already familiar with Fuller, his works, and the controversies he was involved in. While it could serve as an introductory work, it may prove to be a difficult read for the uninitiated.

Regardless of the book's density, it is a definitive work in clarifying some of the confusion surrounding Fuller and his thought, and, while speaking to a specific context within the Southern Baptist Convention, will prove to be useful to any and all who are interested in the thought and theology of the man who was described in his funeral sermon as being "perhaps the most judicious and able theological writer that ever belonged to our [i.e., the Particular Baptist] denomination" (p. 16).

Jordan A. Senécal
Library and Learning Centre Director
Heritage College and Seminary, Cambridge, ON

Baiyu Andrew Song, ed., *Public Worship Considered & Enforced*, British Baptist Classics Series (Peterborough, ON: H&E, 2020), xx + 71 pages.

Keeping the original title, yet updating some of the language, Baiyu Andrew Song equips Joseph Kinghorn's short treatise with the English Standard Version Bible. The title, *Public Worship Considered and Enforced* (1800), may feel archaic to some; however, because words can change meaning over centuries, one may find Samuel Johnson's 1755 definition of the word *enforced* helpful. As a passive participle, *enforced* meant "strengthened; gained by force; provoked to action; compelled; urged; carried into effect." So, the arguments for public worship contained in this short treatise are not only *considered* but also *strengthened*. As such, the principles are also intended to *compel* and *urge* the reader to increase their participation on the Lord's Day with the gathered body of Christ.

Matthew Boswell's "Foreword" serves to connect Joseph Kinghorn's passion for public worship to the relentless Baptist pursuit for a spiritual liturgy, as well as connect to Song's passion to assist modern readers to be acquainted with Joseph Kinghorn. In the editor's "Introduction," Song acts as a tour guide through an art gallery. Song encourages us to examine an old print of about fifteen Georgian-era ministers involved in foreign missions. Pointing us to subtle cues such as posture and gesture, Song provides a rich context of controversy and cooperation in long-eighteenth-century Baptist life. With rich footnotes, Kinghorn's upbringing is provided so that an unacquainted reader may have context, beginning with his father David Kinghorn. Following in his father's footsteps as a Baptist minister, Joseph would become the pastor of St. Mary's Baptist Chapel at Norwich and serve for forty-three years. From the introduction, the book progresses to the original preface, six chapters, and two appendices. The first appendix contains a chronology of Kinghorn's other publications. This work is the second work of twenty-three in total. The second appendix houses an untitled poem written by his father, David Kinghorn, demonstrating his rich spiritual heritage.

Each chapter begins with a short proposition, which is then, either expounded upon or proved. Public worship is asserted as "a Creature's Duty" in the first chapter. From the earliest days of the creation, man has been prepared for the law of Sabbath rest. This prescribed rest was for all classes of people, which has been "a token of our dependence and gratitude" through the ages (p. 29). Public worship is to remind, not only of God's character, but our own condition. Thus, chapter two shows how we can be discipled by the spirituality of others around us. In the third chapter, the gathered body is "a Means of Witness." Through the promotion of religious knowledge every generation and class of persons may increase the influence of God's kingdom, just as "ears of corn in a field; when only a few are strongly moved, the motion is communicated to many more" (pg. 40). Public worship has consequence of blessing to a Christian who participates regularly in it. In taking up one's cross and following Christ, one finds that companionship in the journey most edifying and comforting. When the Christian is in the "society of good men" (pg. 44), they find that they are much more able to endure. In the fifth chapter, public worship is said to be the revelation of the city of God. Each Christian is necessary for the daily production of an economy of God's love and grace in this world. Several pertinent applications are made in the sixth and last chapter. Others are watching you. Be punctual and polite. Prioritize the assembly no matter where you relocate. Recognize the end for which public worship exists—to know Christ.

Because of a resurgence of interest in Baptist ecclesiology in the past decade, this book will likely have a good hearing. Pastors will also want to pick this volume up, so that they might encourage a lax society to prioritize public worship. Public worship is not just a duty, but also for the good and delight of God's people. The principles in this short book, if part of pastoral preaching, may encourage young families to lay-out the shoes the night before. Baiyu Andrew Song's restored volume on the value of public worship demonstrates how meager a livestream substitute really is.

John S. Banks
PhD cand., Vrije Universiteit Amsterdam

Short Notices

Nigel Wheeler, *The Pastoral Priorities of 18th Century Baptists: An Examination of Andrew Fuller's Ordination Sermons* (Peterborough, ON: H&E Academic, 2021), xv+225 pages.

Andrew Fuller was a rigorously thoughtful and biblical practitioner of pastoral ministry. The frequency with which he was asked to preach ordination sermons bears witness to the confidence his contemporary seasoned ministers had in him. Nigel Wheeler's examination of these ordination sermons in the light of prevailing Particular Baptist theological and pastoral interests is richly rewarding in at least three ways.

First, we find Andrew Fuller's deep and biblically-founded spirituality expressed in pastoral ministry beneficial to the church in giving voice to the Bible, to confessional theology, and to truth-founded Christian experience. Second, Wheeler lays to rest any false notions that Fuller's corrective emphases on some issues of evangelism and the duty of repentance and faith led into theological shallowness or even infidelity. Wheeler notes that Fuller's deep polemical awareness of the devastating impact of the infidelities of the day sealed his convictions as a clearly orthodox and confessional Particular Baptist. Even so did he admonish pastoral candidates in these deeply serious convictions. Evangelism with a deep sense of oughtness was not a mere pragmatic technique, but a deeply biblical stewardship related to the glory of God as the chief end of man.

Third, Wheeler demonstrates Fuller's mature and unwavering loyalty to historic Particular Baptist concerns about the stewardship involved in pastoral ministry. The "nature and goals of their theological priorities remained essentially the same." He gives this insightful summary of the lesson from this comparison of ordination sermons: "For as the priorities of a culture change so does the emphatic expression of certain aspects of a fixed theological dogma which is inherently designed to communicate an unchanging message to an ever-changing world." This book is a profoundly helpful analysis of a profoundly insightful person giving biblically-grounded expression to an eternally significant calling.

Tom Nettles
Emeritus Professor of Church History
The Southern Baptist Theological Seminary

Jeremy Walker, *On the Side of God: The Life and Labors of Andrew Fuller* (Conway, AR: Free Grace Press, 2020), 115 pages.

This attractively-produced book captures in a relatively small compass the essential details of Andrew Fuller's life and pastoral ministry. The first half of the book, comprising six chapters, outlines the life of Fuller (p. 13–64). The second half of the book, made up of four chapters, is a digest of Fuller's work as a pastor. What is especially helpful about both sections of this book is both their readability and their recognition that, although Fuller lived in quite a different world than that of the modern West, his writings and witness still have much to teach us. In a significant measure, Walker would argue, this is due to Fuller's biblicism that is, his determination to make the Bible his "decisive rule … for his message and models, for his modes and methods, for his manner and matter" (p. 78–79). Walker also shows that Fuller's genuine humility and pastoral love for people (p. 58, 94, 112–113) make him a tremendous "model of a Christian man and minister" (p. 88). Of course, Walker knows that Fuller had his imperfections and failings (p. 58–62), yet he is also aware that the Bible encourages God's people to imitate the lives of the righteous, and there is no doubt that Fuller's is such a one.

Michael A.G. Haykin
Chair and Professor of Church History
The Southern Baptist Theological Seminary

THE T.V. HAYKIN ESSAY PRIZE

The Andrew Fuller Center for Baptist Studies is pleased to announce the launching of a new annual essay competition in memory of Mrs. T.V. Haykin (1933–1976). The T.V. Haykin Essay Prize seeks to recognize and reward outstanding female Christian researchers in Baptist history and thought.

The T.V. Haykin Essay Prize aims to encourage submissions from female graduate and doctoral students from all over the globe and early career researchers who are within five years of obtaining their PhD. The essay will be on any topic related to the English Particular Baptist history and thought in the long eighteenth century (ca.1689–1834). It should be around 5,000 words (including footnotes following the Chicago-Turabian style) in length. The editorial board of *The Journal of Andrew Fuller Studies* will review all submissions to select the T.V. Haykin Essay Prize winner.

The winner will receive:
- Publication of the winning essay in the Journal of Andrew Fuller Studies;
- $500 (Canadian currency) cash award

Competition Rules:
- Entries should be submitted to bsong@heritagecs.edu before November 30, 2021.
- Entries submitted to the T.V. Haykin Essay Prize must not be under consideration for publication elsewhere.
- The winner of the T.V. Haykin Essay Prize will be required to prove their academic status.

CENTER *for* BAPTIST STUDIES
at THE SOUTHERN BAPTIST THEOLOGICAL SEMINARY

CENTER *for* BAPTIST STUDIES
at THE SOUTHERN BAPTIST THEOLOGICAL SEMINARY

The Andrew Fuller Center for Baptist Studies, located at The Southern Baptist Theological Seminary in Louisville, Kentucky, seeks to promote the study of Baptist history as well as theological reflection on the contemporary significance of that history. The center is named in honor of Andrew Fuller (1754–1815), the late eighteenth- and early nineteenth- century English Baptist pastor and theologian, who played a key role in opposing aberrant thought in his day as well as being instrumental in the founding and early years of the Baptist Missionary Society. Fuller was a close friend and theological mentor of William Carey, one of the pioneers of that society.

The Andrew Fuller Center holds an annual two-day conference in September that examines various aspects of Baptist history and thought. It also supports the publication of the critical edition of the Works of Andrew Fuller, and from time to time, other works in Baptist history. The Center seeks to play a role in the mentoring of junior scholars interested in studying Baptist history.

andrewfullercenter.org

DE GRUYTER

The Andrew Fuller Works Project
It is with deep gratitude to God that The Andrew Fuller Center for Baptist Studies announces that the publishing house of Walter de Gruyter, with head offices in Berlin and Boston, has committed itself to the publication of a modern critical edition of the entire corpus of Andrew Fuller's published and unpublished works. Walter de Gruyter has been synonymous with high-quality, landmark publications in both the humanities and sciences for more than 260 years. The preparation of a critical edition of Fuller's works, part of the work of the Andrew Fuller Center, was first envisioned in 2004. It is expected that this edition this edition will comprise seventeen volumes.

The importance of the project
The controlling objective of The Works of Andrew Fuller Project is to preserve and accurately transmit the text of Fuller's writings. The editors are committed to the finest scholarly standards for textual transcription, editing, and annotation. Transmitting these texts is a vital task since Fuller's writings, not only for their volume, extent, and scope, but for their enduring importance, are major documents in both the Baptist story and the larger history of British Dissent.

From a merely human perspective, if Fuller's theological works had not been written, William Carey would not have gone to India. Fuller's theology was the mainspring behind the formation and early development of the Baptist Missionary Society, the first foreign missionary society created by the Evangelical Revival of the last half of the eighteenth century and the missionary society under whose auspices Carey went to India. Very soon, other missionary societies were established, and a new era in missions had begun as the Christian faith was increasingly spread outside of the West, to the regions of Africa and Asia. Carey was most visible at the fountainhead of this movement. Fuller, though not so visible, was utterly vital to its genesis.

andrewfullercenter.org/the-andrew-fuller-works-project

H&E Publishing is a Canadian evangelical publishing company located out of Peterborough, Ontario. We exist to provide Christ-exalting, Gospel-centred, and Bible-saturated content aimed to show God to be as glorious and worthy as He truly is.

hesedandemet.com

www.ingramcontent.com/pod-product-compliance
Lightning Source LLC
Chambersburg PA
CBHW030912080526
44589CB00010B/265